Collins

5 Minute Maths Mastery

Year 2

Chief editor: Zhou Jieying
Consultant: Fan Lianghuo

CONTENTS

HOW TO USE THIS BOOK

The best way to help children to achieve mastery in maths is to give them lots and lots of practice in the key facts and skills.

Written by maths mastery experts, this series will help children to become fluent in number facts, and help them to recall them quickly – both are essential to mastering maths.

This photocopiable resource saves time with ready-to-practise questions that comprehensively cover the number curriculum for Year 2. It contains 80 topic-based tests, each 5 minutes long, to help children build up their mathematical fluency.

Each test is divided into three Steps:

- **Step 1: Warm-up (1 minute)**
  This exercise helps children to revise maths they should already know and gives them preparation for Step 2.
- **Step 2: Rapid calculation ($2\frac{1}{2}$ minutes)**
  This exercise requires children to answer a set of questions focused on the topic area being tested.
- **Step 3: Challenge ($1\frac{1}{2}$ minutes)**
  This is a more testing exercise designed to stretch the mental abilities of children.

Some of the tests also include a Tip to help children answer questions of a particular type.

Children should attempt to answer as many questions as possible in the time allowed at each Step. Answers are provided at the back of the book.

To help to measure progress, each test includes boxes for recording the date, the total score obtained and the total time taken.

ACKNOWLEDGEMENTS

The authors and publisher are grateful to the copyright holders for permission to use quoted materials and images.

All images are © HarperCollins*Publishers* Ltd and © Shutterstock.com

Every effort has been made to trace copyright holders and obtain their permission for the use of copyright material. The authors and publisher will gladly receive information enabling them to rectify any error or omission in subsequent editions. All facts are correct at time of going to press.

Published by Collins in association with East China Normal University Press

Collins
An imprint of HarperCollins*Publishers*
1 London Bridge Street
London SE1 9GF

ISBN: 978-0-00-831115-5

First published 2019

10 9 8 7 6 5 4 3 2 1

British Library Cataloguing in Publication Data.

A CIP record of this book is available from the British Library.

Publisher: Fiona McGlade
Consultant: Fan Lianghuo
Authors: Zhou Jieying, Xu Jing and Yao Lu
Editors: Ni Ming and Xu Huiping
Contributor: Paul Hodge
Project Management and Editorial: Richard Toms, Lauren Murray and Marie Taylor
Cover Design: Sarah Duxbury
Inside Concept Design: Paul Oates and Ian Wrigley
Layout: Jouve India Private Limited

Printed by CPI Group (UK) Ltd, Croydon

FSC™ www.fsc.org
MIX
Paper from responsible source
FSC® C007454

This book is produced from independently certified FSC™ paper to ensure responsible forest management.

For more information visit: www.harpercollins.co.uk/green

Date: ____________________

Day of Week: ____________________

Addition and subtraction of numbers up to 20 (1)

1

STEP 1 (1 min) Warm-up

Start the timer

Answer these.

8 + 5 = ☐	11 − 2 = ☐	6 + 9 = ☐	10 − 8 = ☐
12 − 6 = ☐	0 + 13 = ☐	15 + 5 = ☐	20 − 10 = ☐
9 + 0 + 8 = ☐	15 − 8 − 2 = ☐		

STEP 2 (2.5 min) Rapid calculation

Start the timer

Answer these.

14 + 6 = ☐	17 − 8 = ☐	9 + 8 = ☐	18 + 0 = ☐
7 + 5 = ☐	4 + 17 = ☐	9 + 11 = ☐	16 − 8 = ☐
8 + 10 = ☐	16 − 4 = ☐	11 + 0 = ☐	15 − 15 = ☐
15 − 0 = ☐	11 + 8 = ☐	15 − 8 = ☐	7 + 7 = ☐
17 − 9 = ☐	2 + 5 + 8 = ☐	7 + 5 − 7 = ☐	8 − 6 + 8 = ☐

STEP 3 (1.5 min) Challenge

Start the timer

Fill in the missing numbers.

8 + ☐ = 16	☐ − 6 = 5	4 + ☐ = 13	14 − ☐ = 6
☐ + 10 = 12	7 + ☐ = 13	☐ − 7 = 7	15 − ☐ = 9

Time spent: ________ min ________ sec. Total: ________ out of 38

2 Addition and subtraction of numbers up to 20 (2)

Date: __________

Day of Week: __________

STEP 1 (1 min) Warm-up

Start the timer

Answer these.

4 + 9 = ☐	15 – 8 = ☐	17 + 0 = ☐	14 – 9 = ☐
8 + 5 = ☐	13 – 8 = ☐	13 – 5 = ☐	13 – 0 = ☐
3 + 0 + 7 = ☐	12 – 4 – 6 = ☐		

STEP 2 (2.5 min) Rapid calculation

Start the timer

Answer these.

14 – 8 = ☐	9 + 8 = ☐	6 + 7 = ☐	0 + 11 = ☐
5 + 11 = ☐	17 – 4 = ☐	8 + 12 = ☐	14 – 7 = ☐
10 + 9 = ☐	10 – 8 = ☐	9 + 7 = ☐	7 + 9 = ☐
16 – 7 = ☐	16 – 9 = ☐	8 + 8 = ☐	5 + 8 = ☐
18 – 9 = ☐	4 + 3 + 7 = ☐	6 + 8 – 6 = ☐	9 – 9 + 9 = ☐

STEP 3 (1.5 min) Challenge

Start the timer

Fill in the missing numbers.

☐ + 2 = 16	☐ – 4 = 5	4 + ☐ = 13	6 – ☐ = 6
☐ + 8 = 12	9 + ☐ = 17	☐ – 11 = 7	☐ + 6 = 15

Time spent: _____ min _____ sec. Total: _____ out of 38

Date: ____________

Day of Week: ____________

Addition and subtraction of numbers up to 20 (3)

STEP 1 (1 min) Warm-up

Start the timer

Add and subtract these amounts of money.

3p + 8p =	£5 + £6 =
20p – 5p =	£7 – £5 =
14p + 3p =	£13 + £6 =
13p – 7p =	£18 – £7 =
12p + 5p =	£8 + £9 =

STEP 2 (2.5 min) Rapid calculation

Start the timer

Add and subtract these lengths.

12 m – 8 m =	8 m + 11 m =
7 m + 5 m =	5 m + 13 m =
11 m – 4 m =	15 m – 8 m =
2 m + 13 m =	13 m – 12 m =
16 m – 11 m =	9 m + 9 m =
15 cm – 7 cm =	14 cm + 6 cm =
6 cm + 12 cm =	8 cm + 8 cm =
18 cm – 9 cm =	14 cm – 7 cm =
10 cm + 6 cm =	19 cm – 17 cm =
12 cm – 5 cm =	18 cm – 0 cm =

STEP 3 (1.5 min) Challenge

Start the timer

Fill in the missing lengths.

☐ + 5 cm = 17 cm   ☐ – 6 cm = 6 cm   4 cm + ☐ = 11 cm

12 cm – ☐ = 3 cm   ☐ + 9 m = 13 m   5 m + ☐ = 14 m

☐ – 6 m = 5 m   ☐ + 7 m = 12 m

Time spent: ______ min ______ sec. Total: ______ out of 38

4 Comparison

Date: ______________________

Day of Week: ______________________

STEP 1 (1 min) Warm-up

Start the timer

Answer these.

5 + 10 = □	13 − 3 = □	10 + 9 = □	17 − 7 = □
7 + 7 = □	10 + 5 = □	10 + 3 = □	19 − 9 = □
17 − 10 = □	14 − 7 = □		

STEP 2 (2.5 min) Rapid calculation

Start the timer

Fill in each box with **>**, **<** or **=**.

14 − 8 □ 14	3 + 8 □ 8	5 + 5 □ 10	11 − 6 □ 11
11 □ 10 + 3	11 □ 10 + 2	11 □ 10 + 1	11 □ 10 + 0
11 □ 12 − 0	11 □ 12 − 1	11 □ 12 − 2	11 □ 12 − 3
11 □ 11 + 0	11 □ 11 − 0	11 □ 11 − 1	11 □ 11 + 1

STEP 3 (1.5 min) Challenge

Start the timer

Find the largest number or digit that can be filled in each box.

□2 < 16	9□ < 100	□7 < 98	65 > 6□
□ + 2 < 16	9 + □ < 15	□ − 3 < 13	17 − □ > 6

Time spent: ________ min ________ sec. Total: ________ out of 34

Date: ____________________

Day of Week: ____________________

Adding a whole tens to a two-digit number (1)

STEP 1 (1 min) Warm-up

Start the timer

Answer these.

30 + 40 = ☐ 70 + 20 = ☐ 50 + 30 = ☐ 80 + 10 = ☐

70 + 2 = ☐ 90 + 5 = ☐ 80 + 4 = ☐ 90 + 7 = ☐

STEP 2 (2.5 min) Rapid calculation

Start the timer

Answer these.

32 + 40 = ☐ 75 + 20 = ☐ 54 + 30 = ☐ 87 + 10 = ☐

77 + 20 = ☐ 58 + 30 = ☐ 30 + 63 = ☐ 30 + 47 = ☐

25 + 60 = ☐ 51 + 40 = ☐ 10 + 39 = ☐ 52 + 30 = ☐

60 + 12 = ☐ 40 + 15 = ☐ 39 + 10 = ☐ 30 + 25 = ☐

70 + 13 = ☐ 30 + 56 = ☐ 51 + 20 = ☐ 50 + 50 = ☐

STEP 3 (1.5 min) Challenge

Start the timer

Fill in the missing numbers.

30 + ☐ = 60 ☐ + 40 = 80 ☐ + 20 = 40

30 + ☐ = 78 7 + ☐ = 67 ☐ + 40 = 69

25 + ☐ = 55 30 + ☐ = 65 98 = ☐ + 50

Time spent: ________ min ________ sec. Total: ________ out of 37

6 Adding a whole tens to a two-digit number (2)

Date: ______________________

Day of Week: ______________________

STEP 1 (1 min) Warm-up

Start the timer

Answer these.

10 + 5 = ☐ 50 + 3 = ☐ 1 + 70 = ☐ 3 + 30 = ☐

50 + 8 = ☐ 27 + 30 = ☐ 40 + 19 = ☐ 31 + 60 = ☐

STEP 2 (2.5 min) Rapid calculation

Start the timer

1. Answer these.

28 + 30 = ☐ 11 + 20 = ☐ 10 + 85 = ☐ 36 + 30 = ☐

30 + 13 = ☐ 54 + 20 = ☐ 17 + 80 = ☐ 25 + 20 = ☐

20 + 71 = ☐ 50 + 40 = ☐

2. Fill in each box with **>**, **<** or **=**.

38 + 60 ☐ 88 66 + 10 ☐ 86 27 + 20 ☐ 67 84 + 10 ☐ 54

53 + 30 ☐ 63 15 + 70 ☐ 85 78 + 20 ☐ 88 14 + 70 ☐ 84

STEP 3 (1.5 min) Challenge

Start the timer

Fill in the missing numbers.

42 + ☐ = 82 ☐ + 10 = 45 32 + ☐ = 52

33 + ☐ = 63 20 + ☐ = 94 ☐ + 52 = 82

34 + ☐ = 84 24 + ☐ = 54 67 = ☐ + 30

Time spent: ________ min ________ sec. Total: ________ out of 35

Date: ______________________

Day of Week: ______________________

Adding a whole tens to a two-digit number (3)

STEP 1 (1 min) Warm-up

Start the timer

Add these amounts of money.

£10 + £7 =	16p + 20p =
£40 + £6 =	30p + 18p =
£3 + £80 =	22p + 70p =
£9 + £50 =	10p + 87p =
£60 + £5 =	40p + 30p =

STEP 2 (2.5 min) Rapid calculation

Start the timer

1. Add these lengths.

17 m + 40 m =	50 cm + 17 cm =
15 m + 60 m =	44 cm + 40 cm =
10 m + 75 m =	12 cm + 70 cm =
43 m + 20 m =	35 cm + 30 cm =

2. Fill in each box with **>**, **<** or **=**.

£26 + £50 ☐ £77 | £43 + £20 ☐ £63 | £38 + £50 ☐ £89

£72 + £20 ☐ £81 | 21p + 20p ☐ 41p | 54p + 40p ☐ 93p

57p + 30p ☐ 87p | 17p + 80p ☐ 98p

STEP 3 (1.5 min) Challenge

Start the timer

Fill in the missing lengths.

36 m + ☐ = 56 m | ☐ + 20 m = 62 m | 44 m + ☐ = 84 m

61 cm + ☐ = 91 cm | 50 cm + ☐ = 99 cm | ☐ + 27 cm = 67 cm

55 m + ☐ = 65 m | 22 cm + ☐ = 42 cm | 86 m = ☐ + 30 m

Time spent: ________ min ________ sec. Total: ________ out of 35

8 Subtracting a whole tens from a two-digit number (1)

Date: ______________________

Day of Week: ______________________

STEP 1 (1 min) Warm-up

Start the timer

Answer these.

60 – 20 = ☐ 80 – 10 = ☐ 90 – 70 = ☐ 50 – 20 = ☐

40 + 1 = ☐ 70 + 7 = ☐ 20 + 6 = ☐ 30 + 4 = ☐

STEP 2 (2.5 min) Rapid calculation

Start the timer

Answer these.

61 – 20 = ☐ 87 – 10 = ☐ 96 – 70 = ☐ 54 – 20 = ☐

77 – 20 = ☐ 58 – 30 = ☐ 63 – 30 = ☐ 47 – 20 = ☐

65 – 20 = ☐ 51 – 40 = ☐ 39 – 10 = ☐ 52 – 30 = ☐

62 – 60 = ☐ 95 – 50 = ☐ 85 – 40 = ☐ 35 – 30 = ☐

97 – 90 = ☐ 91 – 80 = ☐ 51 – 20 = ☐ 50 – 50 = ☐

STEP 3 (1.5 min) Challenge

Start the timer

Fill in the missing numbers.

93 – ☐ = 60 ☐ – 50 = 28 ☐ – 70 = 12

86 – ☐ = 16 45 – ☐ = 5 ☐ – 50 = 46

88 – ☐ = 38 99 – ☐ = 69 37 = ☐ – 20

Time spent: ________ min ________ sec. Total: ________ out of 37

Date: ______________________

Day of Week: ______________________

Subtracting a whole tens from a two-digit number (2)

STEP 1 (1 min) Warm-up

Start the timer

Answer these.

10 – 5 = ☐ 50 – 3 = ☐ 70 – 1 = ☐ 30 – 3 = ☐

50 – 8 = ☐ 78 – 30 = ☐ 59 – 40 = ☐ 69 – 30 = ☐

STEP 2 (2.5 min) Rapid calculation

Start the timer

1. Answer these.

81 – 10 = ☐ 95 – 40 = ☐ 84 – 10 = ☐ 56 – 30 = ☐

58 – 20 = ☐ 47 – 40 = ☐ 99 – 70 = ☐ 61 – 50 = ☐

99 – 90 = ☐ 50 – 40 = ☐

2. Fill in each box with **>**, **<** or **=**.

99 – 50 ☐ 59 56 – 50 ☐ 16 73 – 20 ☐ 33 92 – 40 ☐ 62

86 – 60 ☐ 16 75 – 30 ☐ 55 72 – 40 ☐ 22 93 – 20 ☐ 53

STEP 3 (1.5 min) Challenge

Start the timer

Fill in the missing numbers.

37 – ☐ = 7 61 – ☐ = 31 ☐ – 50 = 19

91 – ☐ = 21 ☐ – 20 = 42 ☐ – 20 = 19

93 – ☐ = 43 87 – ☐ = 37 25 = ☐ – 30

Time spent: ________ min ________ sec. Total: ________ out of 35

10 Subtracting a whole tens from a two-digit number (3)

Date: ____________________

Day of Week: ____________________

STEP 1 (1 min) Warm-up

Start the timer

Subtract these amounts.

£30 – £5 =	77p – 20p =
£40 – £4 =	83p – 40p =
£60 – £2 =	48p – 20p =
£70 – £6 =	95p – 80p =
£50 – £9 =	64p – 50p =

STEP 2 (2.5 min) Rapid calculation

Start the timer

1. Subtract these lengths.

42 m – 30 m =	57 cm – 30 cm =
88 m – 50 m =	96 cm – 70 cm =
69 m – 10 m =	35 cm – 30 cm =
71 m – 60 m =	99 cm – 80 cm =

2. Fill in each box with **>**, **<** or **=**.

£47 – £10 ☐ £38 £36 – £20 ☐ £15 £71 – £40 ☐ £31

£95 – £70 ☐ £35 78p – 30p ☐ 49p 65p – 50p ☐ 5p

64p – 40p ☐ 24p 88p – 80p ☐ 9p

STEP 3 (1.5 min) Challenge

Start the timer

Fill in the missing lengths.

34 m – ☐ = 8 m 55 m – ☐ = 28 m ☐ – 40 m = 29 m

86 cm – ☐ = 33 cm ☐ – 40 cm = 22 cm ☐ – 60 cm = 33 cm

67 m – ☐ = 24 m 66 cm – ☐ = 48 cm 35 m = ☐ – 20 m

Time spent: ________ min ________ sec. Total: ________ out of 35

Date: ____________________

Day of Week: ____________________

Adding a one-digit number to a two-digit number (1)

11

STEP 1 (1 min) Warm-up

Start the timer

Answer these.

6 + 2 = ☐	5 + 4 = ☐	2 + 5 = ☐	3 + 6 = ☐
40 + 20 = ☐	70 + 10 = ☐	30 + 50 = ☐	7 + 40 = ☐

STEP 2 (2.5 min) Rapid calculation

Start the timer

Answer these.

83 + 6 = ☐	51 + 4 = ☐	70 + 9 = ☐	63 + 6 = ☐
6 + 52 = ☐	41 + 8 = ☐	7 + 82 = ☐	6 + 33 = ☐
5 + 33 = ☐	3 + 66 = ☐	51 + 6 = ☐	41 + 5 = ☐
60 + 8 = ☐	20 + 9 = ☐	40 + 7 = ☐	50 + 9 = ☐
66 + 2 = ☐	25 + 4 = ☐	42 + 5 = ☐	53 + 6 = ☐

STEP 3 (1.5 min) Challenge

Start the timer

Fill in the missing numbers.

5 + ☐ = 65	☐ + 8 = 98	☐ + 9 = 69
6 + ☐ = 77	7 + ☐ = 58	☐ + 4 = 47
5 + ☐ = 45	3 + ☐ = 84	58 = ☐ + 52

Time spent: ________ min ________ sec. Total: ________ out of 37

12 Adding a one-digit number to a two-digit number (2)

Date: ____________

Day of Week: ____________

STEP 1 (1 min) Warm-up

Start the timer

Answer these.

70 + 6 = ☐ 10 + 80 = ☐ 2 + 90 = ☐ 50 + 40 = ☐

4 + 13 = ☐ 33 + 6 = ☐ 3 + 31 = ☐ 55 + 4 = ☐

STEP 2 (2.5 min) Rapid calculation

Start the timer

1. Answer these.

9 + 40 = ☐ 51 + 7 = ☐ 75 + 3 = ☐ 62 + 6 = ☐ 76 + 3 = ☐

18 + 1 = ☐ 82 + 5 = ☐ 86 + 2 = ☐ 41 + 8 = ☐ 41 + 4 = ☐

2. Fill in each box with **>**, **<** or **=**.

44 + 4 ☐ 42 + 6 25 – 3 ☐ 27 + 2 94 + 5 ☐ 92 + 7

86 + 2 ☐ 83 + 4 73 + 5 ☐ 72 + 6 15 + 3 ☐ 14 + 5

76 + 2 ☐ 71 + 6 82 + 3 ☐ 81 + 7

STEP 3 (1.5 min) Challenge

Start the timer

Fill in the missing numbers.

35 + ☐ = 39 ☐ + 22 = 27 ☐ + 4 = 37

62 + ☐ = 68 6 + ☐ = 57 ☐ + 8 = 99

☐ + 42 = 45 63 + ☐ = 68 87 = ☐ + 83

Time spent: ________ min ________ sec. Total: ________ out of 35

Date: ______________________

Day of Week: ______________________

Subtracting a one-digit number from a two-digit number (1)

STEP 1 (1 min) Warm-up

Start the timer

Answer these.

7 − 4 = ☐   9 − 8 = ☐   8 − 3 = ☐   6 − 4 = ☐

50 + 3 = ☐   70 + 1 = ☐   40 + 5 = ☐   90 + 2 = ☐

STEP 2 (2.5 min) Rapid calculation

Start the timer

Answer these.

20 − 6 = ☐   30 − 7 = ☐   48 − 9 = ☐   53 − 8 = ☐

56 − 5 = ☐   82 − 5 = ☐   64 − 6 = ☐   73 − 4 = ☐

61 − 2 = ☐   62 − 3 = ☐   63 − 4 = ☐   64 − 5 = ☐

61 − 9 = ☐   62 − 8 = ☐   63 − 7 = ☐   64 − 6 = ☐

57 − 4 = ☐   79 − 8 = ☐   48 − 3 = ☐   96 − 4 = ☐

STEP 3 (1.5 min) Challenge

Start the timer

Fill in the missing numbers.

51 − ☐ = 9   82 − ☐ = 5   46 − ☐ = 8

62 − ☐ = 7   64 − ☐ = 8   98 − ☐ = 8

3 = 91 − ☐   5 = 73 − ☐   72 − ☐ = 62 + 8

Time spent: ________ min ________ sec. Total: ________ out of 37

14

Subtracting a one-digit number from a two-digit number (2)

Date: ______

Day of Week: ______

STEP 1 (1 min) Warm-up

Start the timer

Answer these.

53 – 8 = ☐ 31 – 6 = ☐ 46 – 5 = ☐ 76 – 8 = ☐

92 – 7 = ☐ 20 – 1 = ☐ 31 – 2 = ☐ 42 – 3 = ☐

STEP 2 (2.5 min) Rapid calculation

Start the timer

1. Answer these.

29 – 6 = ☐ 85 – 7 = ☐ 41 – 5 = ☐ 90 – 2 = ☐

63 – 6 = ☐ 50 – 5 = ☐ 72 – 3 = ☐ 34 – 9 = ☐

53 – 4 = ☐ 64 – 5 = ☐

2. Fill in each box with **>**, **<** or **=**.

56 – 7 ☐ 51 74 – 6 ☐ 71 38 – 4 ☐ 33 50 – 8 ☐ 43

36 – 7 ☐ 35 61 – 9 ☐ 52 72 – 6 ☐ 66 71 – 8 ☐ 62

STEP 3 (1.5 min) Challenge

Start the timer

Fill in the missing numbers.

81 – ☐ = 75 ☐ – 9 = 73 52 – ☐ = 45

☐ – 4 = 21 33 – ☐ = 25 69 – ☐ = 62

50 = ☐ – 7 40 = 49 – ☐ ☐ – 8 = 18 + 2

Time spent: ______ min ______ sec. Total: ______ out of 35

Date: ______________________

Day of Week: ______________________

Adding or subtracting a one-digit number to or from a two-digit number (1)

15

STEP 1 (1 min) Warm-up

Start the timer

Answer these.

53 + 8 = ☐	31 + 6 = ☐	46 + 5 = ☐	76 + 8 = ☐
92 + 0 = ☐	30 – 2 = ☐	56 – 7 = ☐	75 – 9 = ☐

STEP 2 (2.5 min) Rapid calculation

Start the timer

Answer these.

67 – 8 = ☐	63 + 5 = ☐	28 + 7 = ☐	73 – 5 = ☐
43 – 9 = ☐	25 + 9 = ☐	66 + 7 = ☐	90 – 9 = ☐
70 – 0 = ☐	70 + 0 = ☐	78 – 8 = ☐	51 + 9 = ☐
73 – 7 = ☐	50 – 2 = ☐	27 + 3 = ☐	64 + 6 = ☐
81 – 4 = ☐	35 – 0 = ☐		

STEP 3 (1.5 min) Challenge

Start the timer

Fill in the missing numbers.

35 + ☐ = 40	☐ – 35 = 5	40 – ☐ = 35
☐ – 8 = 65	☐ + 76 = 85	72 – ☐ = 65
53 = ☐ + 47	17 = 24 – ☐	☐ – 22 = 60

Time spent: ________ min ________ sec. Total: ________ out of 35

16 Adding or subtracting a one-digit number to or from a two-digit number (2)

Date: ______

Day of Week: ______

STEP 1 (1 min) Warm-up

Start the timer

Answer these.

1. 67 + 6 = ☐

67 + 3 + 3 = ☐

2. 87 − 8 = ☐

87 − 7 − 1 = ☐

3. 9 + 55 = ☐

5 + 55 + 4 = ☐

4. 74 − 7 = ☐

74 − 4 − 3 = ☐

5. 68 − 9 = ☐

68 − 8 − 1 = ☐

STEP 2 (2.5 min) Rapid calculation

Start the timer

Answer these.

89 − 9 = ☐	57 + 6 = ☐	63 + 7 = ☐	81 − 5 = ☐
89 + 9 = ☐	57 − 6 = ☐	63 − 7 = ☐	81 + 5 = ☐
43 − 6 = ☐	73 + 8 = ☐	64 − 8 = ☐	4 + 58 = ☐
43 − 9 = ☐	81 − 8 = ☐	56 + 6 = ☐	6 + 58 = ☐
4 + 37 = ☐	49 − 7 = ☐	6 + 65 = ☐	39 − 4 = ☐

STEP 3 (1.5 min) Challenge

Start the timer

Fill in the missing numbers.

☐ − 8 = 33	24 + ☐ = 32	73 − ☐ = 66
50 = ☐ + 4	☐ − 9 = 50	92 − ☐ = 90
56 + ☐ = 65	☐ + 63 = 70	72 − ☐ = 64

Time spent: ______ min ______ sec. Total: ______ out of 39

Date: ____________________

Day of Week: ____________________

Adding or subtracting a one-digit number to or from a two-digit number (3)

STEP 1 (1 min) Warm-up

Start the timer

Add and subtract these amounts of money.

£62 + £9 =	60p – 6p =
£46 + £6 =	54p – 8p =
£59 + £8 =	95p – 7p =
£73 + £9 =	77p – 9p =
£85 + £7 =	42p – 5p =

STEP 2 (2.5 min) Rapid calculation

Start the timer

Add and subtract these lengths.

55 m – 7 m =	90 m – 9 m =
43 m + 8 m =	50 m + 8 m =
67 m + 7 m =	72 m – 5 m =
73 m – 6 m =	61 m + 9 m =
23 cm – 8 cm =	44 cm – 5 cm =
36 cm + 7 cm =	70 cm – 5 cm =
54 cm + 8 cm =	58 cm + 4 cm =
80 cm – 6 cm =	89 cm + 9 cm =
91 cm – 5 cm =	93 cm + 6 cm =

STEP 3 (1.5 min) Challenge

Start the timer

Fill in the missing amounts.

£42 + ☐ = £50   ☐ – £28 = £10   £60 – ☐ = £25

☐ – £7 = £29   ☐ + £56 = £85   £82 – ☐ = £48

£39 = ☐ + £17   £26 = £46 – ☐   ☐ – £32 = £40

Time spent: ______ min ______ sec. Total: ______ out of 37

18 Adding a two-digit number to a two-digit number (1)

Date: ______________________

Day of Week: ______________________

STEP 1 (1 min) Warm-up

Start the timer

Answer these.

3 + 4 = ☐   5 + 3 = ☐   30 + 50 = ☐   20 + 60 = ☐

40 + 50 = ☐   20 + 70 = ☐   10 + 30 = ☐   34 + 52 = ☐

STEP 2 (2.5 min) Rapid calculation

Start the timer

Answer these.

21 + 70 = ☐   30 + 57 = ☐   50 + 35 = ☐   74 + 10 = ☐

41 + 54 = ☐   12 + 73 = ☐   21 + 24 = ☐   64 + 15 = ☐

42 + 25 = ☐   23 + 73 = ☐   86 + 11 = ☐   71 + 13 = ☐

21 + 21 = ☐   43 + 43 = ☐   34 + 34 = ☐   13 + 13 = ☐

21 + 68 = ☐   43 + 54 = ☐   25 + 73 = ☐   14 + 32 = ☐

STEP 3 (1.5 min) Challenge

Start the timer

Fill in the missing numbers.

11 + 22 = ☐   22 + 33 = ☐   33 + 44 = ☐

32 + 23 = ☐   61 + 16 = ☐   27 + 72 = ☐

18 + ☐ = 88   51 + ☐ = 79   66 = ☐ + 44

Time spent: ________ min ________ sec. Total: ________ out of 37

Date: ______________________

Day of Week: ______________________

Adding a two-digit number to a two-digit number (2)

STEP 1 (1 min) Warm-up

Start the timer

Answer these.

31 + 20 = ☐ 54 + 30 = ☐ 40 + 16 = ☐ 68 + 30 = ☐

40 + 58 = ☐ 17 + 13 = ☐ 73 + 17 = ☐ 55 + 25 = ☐

STEP 2 (2.5 min) Rapid calculation

Start the timer

Answer these.

21 + 59 = ☐ 33 + 57 = ☐ 65 + 15 = ☐ 64 + 16 = ☐

47 + 38 = ☐ 37 + 48 = ☐ 27 + 58 = ☐ 17 + 68 = ☐

49 + 25 = ☐ 25 + 49 = ☐ 76 + 15 = ☐ 16 + 75 = ☐

29 + 29 = ☐ 48 + 48 = ☐ 37 + 37 = ☐ 26 + 26 = ☐

42 + 38 = ☐ 57 + 33 = ☐

STEP 3 (1.5 min) Challenge

Start the timer

Answer these.

19 + 22 = ☐ 28 + 33 = ☐ 37 + 44 = ☐

39 + 13 = ☐ 49 + 23 = ☐ 59 + 33 = ☐

18 + 25 = ☐ 54 + 39 = ☐ 66 + 28 = ☐

Time spent: ________ min ________ sec. Total: ________ out of 35

20 Adding a two-digit number to a two-digit number (3)

Date: ____________________

Day of Week: ____________________

STEP 1 (1 min) Warm-up

Start the timer

Answer these.

31 + 23 = ☐ 54 + 32 = ☐ 43 + 16 = ☐ 68 + 32 = ☐

41 + 58 = ☐ 18 + 13 = ☐ 75 + 17 = ☐ 55 + 29 = ☐

STEP 2 (2.5 min) Rapid calculation

Start the timer

Answer these.

38 + 38 = ☐ 27 + 27 = ☐ 49 + 49 = ☐ 16 + 16 = ☐

67 + 16 = ☐ 57 + 26 = ☐ 47 + 36 = ☐ 37 + 46 = ☐

17 + 15 = ☐ 27 + 25 = ☐ 37 + 35 = ☐ 47 + 45 = ☐

38 + 55 = ☐ 29 + 38 = ☐ 47 + 34 = ☐ 78 + 13 = ☐

46 + 36 = ☐ 52 + 39 = ☐

STEP 3 (1.5 min) Challenge

Start the timer

Answer these.

37 + 16 = ☐ 29 + 57 = ☐ 39 + 36 = ☐

59 + 12 = ☐ 59 + 14 = ☐ 59 + 16 = ☐

38 + 23 = ☐ 38 + 25 = ☐ 38 + 27 = ☐

Time spent: ________ min ________ sec. Total: ________ out of 35

Date: ____________________

Day of Week: ____________________

Adding a two-digit number to a two-digit number (4)

21

STEP 1 (1 min) Warm-up

Start the timer

Answer these.

24 + 42 = ☐ 27 + 72 = ☐ 35 + 53 = ☐ 45 + 54 = ☐

12 + 21 = ☐ 56 + 28 = ☐ 70 + 11 = ☐ 37 + 56 = ☐

STEP 2 (2.5 min) Rapid calculation

Start the timer

Answer these.

17 + 17 = ☐ 27 + 70 = ☐ 53 + 27 = ☐ 37 + 43 = ☐

39 + 25 = ☐ 29 + 35 = ☐ 60 + 37 = ☐ 68 + 18 = ☐

46 + 17 = ☐ 88 + 10 = ☐ 84 + 15 = ☐ 36 + 57 = ☐

46 + 44 = ☐ 51 + 15 = ☐ 67 + 18 = ☐ 72 + 19 = ☐

28 + 42 = ☐ 79 + 19 = ☐

STEP 3 (1.5 min) Challenge

Start the timer

Fill in the missing numbers.

58 + 18 = ☐ 63 + 28 = ☐ 47 + 25 = ☐

☐ + 13 = 40 30 + ☐ = 88 17 + ☐ = 40

46 + ☐ = 87 ☐ + 27 = 65 ☐ + 36 = 91

Time spent: ________ min ________ sec. Total: ________ out of 35

22 Subtracting a two-digit number from a two-digit number (1)

Date: ____________

Day of Week: ____________

STEP 1 (1 min) Warm-up

Start the timer

Answer these.

80 – 70 = ☐ 90 – 30 = ☐ 70 – 20 = ☐ 60 – 40 = ☐

50 – 30 = ☐ 86 – 74 = ☐ 99 – 35 = ☐ 76 – 23 = ☐

STEP 2 (2.5 min) Rapid calculation

Start the timer

Answer these.

56 – 10 = ☐ 38 – 18 = ☐ 50 – 10 = ☐ 97 – 17 = ☐

54 – 41 = ☐ 73 – 12 = ☐ 66 – 33 = ☐ 84 – 42 = ☐

96 – 25 = ☐ 68 – 23 = ☐ 86 – 21 = ☐ 78 – 55 = ☐

79 – 26 = ☐ 43 – 43 = ☐ 49 – 10 = ☐ 62 – 21 = ☐

67 – 42 = ☐ 58 – 37 = ☐

STEP 3 (1.5 min) Challenge

Start the timer

Fill in the missing numbers.

88 – 22 = ☐ 77 – 33 = ☐ 66 – 44 = ☐

88 – 15 = ☐ 78 – 25 = ☐ 68 – 35 = ☐

53 – ☐ = 3 ☐ – 18 = 70 57 = 98 – ☐

Time spent: ________ min ________ sec. Total: ________ out of 35

Date: ______________________

Day of Week: ______________________

Subtracting a two-digit number from a two-digit number (2)

STEP 1 (1 min) Warm-up

Start the timer

Answer these.

31 – 20 = ☐ 54 – 30 = ☐ 40 – 16 = ☐ 68 – 30 = ☐

58 – 40 = ☐ 17 – 13 = ☐ 73 – 23 = ☐ 55 – 25 = ☐

STEP 2 (2.5 min) Rapid calculation

Start the timer

Answer these.

50 – 19 = ☐ 50 – 27 = ☐ 55 – 15 = ☐ 77 – 25 = ☐

76 – 38 = ☐ 58 – 29 = ☐ 78 – 39 = ☐ 98 – 49 = ☐

42 – 13 = ☐ 52 – 23 = ☐ 62 – 33 = ☐ 72 – 43 = ☐

83 – 17 = ☐ 73 – 27 = ☐ 63 – 37 = ☐ 53 – 47 = ☐

42 – 38 = ☐ 57 – 33 = ☐

STEP 3 (1.5 min) Challenge

Start the timer

Answer these.

22 – 13 = ☐ 33 – 14 = ☐ 44 – 15 = ☐

30 – 19 = ☐ 43 – 25 = ☐ 74 – 47 = ☐

65 – 29 = ☐ 71 – 58 = ☐ 83 – 18 = ☐

Time spent: ________ min ________ sec. Total: ________ out of 35

24

Subtracting a two-digit number from a two-digit number (3)

Date: ______

Day of Week: ______

STEP 1 (1 min) Warm-up

Start the timer

Answer these.

30 – 23 = ☐ 54 – 32 = ☐ 43 – 23 = ☐ 68 – 32 = ☐

58 – 41 = ☐ 23 – 18 = ☐ 56 – 28 = ☐ 99 – 99 = ☐

STEP 2 (2.5 min) Rapid calculation

Start the timer

Answer these.

71 – 26 = ☐ 72 – 27 = ☐ 73 – 28 = ☐ 74 – 29 = ☐

93 – 28 = ☐ 75 – 28 = ☐ 63 – 38 = ☐ 53 – 48 = ☐

45 – 27 = ☐ 55 – 49 = ☐ 62 – 38 = ☐ 70 – 35 = ☐

61 – 27 = ☐ 45 – 36 = ☐ 75 – 37 = ☐ 86 – 58 = ☐

74 – 37 = ☐ 36 – 18 = ☐

STEP 3 (1.5 min) Challenge

Start the timer

Answer these.

35 – 18 = ☐ 57 – 28 = ☐ 90 – 45 = ☐

53 – 18 = ☐ 53 – 16 = ☐ 53 – 14 = ☐

42 – 19 = ☐ 42 – 17 = ☐ 42 – 15 = ☐

Time spent: ______ min ______ sec. Total: ______ out of 35

Date: ______________

Day of Week: ______________

Subtracting a two-digit number from a two-digit number (4)

25

STEP 1 (1 min) Warm-up

Start the timer

Answer these.

42 – 24 = ☐ 72 – 27 = ☐ 53 – 35 = ☐ 54 – 45 = ☐

21 – 12 = ☐ 56 – 28 = ☐ 70 – 11 = ☐ 64 – 38 = ☐

STEP 2 (2.5 min) Rapid calculation

Start the timer

Answer these.

33 – 17 = ☐ 33 – 27 = ☐ 33 – 13 = ☐ 23 – 20 = ☐

43 – 26 = ☐ 53 – 19 = ☐ 60 – 37 = ☐ 87 – 28 = ☐

66 – 18 = ☐ 57 – 57 = ☐ 84 – 16 = ☐ 67 – 39 = ☐

71 – 37 = ☐ 51 – 15 = ☐ 67 – 18 = ☐ 72 – 49 = ☐

41 – 19 = ☐ 88 – 88 = ☐

STEP 3 (1.5 min) Challenge

Start the timer

Fill in the missing numbers.

58 – 18 = ☐ 63 – 28 = ☐ 40 – 25 = ☐

☐ – 13 = 40 50 – ☐ = 28 67 – ☐ = 40

97 – ☐ = 58 ☐ – 27 = 65 ☐ – 36 = 51

Time spent: ______ min ______ sec. Total: ______ out of 35

26 Addition and subtraction of two-digit numbers (1)

Date: ____________________

Day of Week: ____________________

STEP 1 (1 min) Warm-up

Start the timer

Answer these.

53 + 20 = ☐ 27 − 8 = ☐ 40 − 14 = ☐ 67 + 30 = ☐

40 + 55 = ☐ 81 − 60 = ☐ 96 − 9 = ☐ 89 + 5 = ☐

STEP 2 (2.5 min) Rapid calculation

Start the timer

Answer these.

21 + 78 = ☐ 57 − 27 = ☐ 53 + 35 = ☐ 74 − 24 = ☐

36 + 54 = ☐ 17 + 73 = ☐ 50 − 29 = ☐ 63 − 36 = ☐

56 + 25 = ☐ 73 − 18 = ☐ 65 + 25 = ☐ 78 − 13 = ☐

51 − 51 = ☐ 49 + 18 = ☐ 75 − 57 = ☐ 68 + 10 = ☐

90 − 18 = ☐ 40 + 40 = ☐

STEP 3 (1.5 min) Challenge

Start the timer

Fill in the missing numbers.

67 − 18 = ☐ 38 + 13 = ☐ 16 + ☐ = 45

18 + 45 = ☐ 85 − 59 = ☐ 71 − ☐ = 35

93 − 78 = ☐ 27 + 25 = ☐ 35 = ☐ − 35

Time spent: ________ min ________ sec. Total: ________ out of 35

Date: ____________________

Day of Week: ____________________

Addition and subtraction of two-digit numbers (2)

STEP 1 (1 min) Warm-up

Start the timer

Answer these.

27 + 10 = ☐   63 – 20 = ☐   46 + 7 = ☐   51 – 3 = ☐

60 – 35 = ☐   65 + 19 = ☐   77 – 39 = ☐   63 + 28 = ☐

STEP 2 (2.5 min) Rapid calculation

Start the timer

Answer these.

44 + 28 = ☐   78 + 18 = ☐   62 – 35 = ☐   71 – 55 = ☐

72 – 28 = ☐   96 – 18 = ☐   27 + 35 = ☐   19 + 52 = ☐

54 – 27 = ☐   30 + 67 = ☐   61 – 44 = ☐   57 + 29 = ☐

58 – 28 = ☐   67 – 10 = ☐   37 + 24 = ☐   28 + 29 = ☐

63 – 28 = ☐   17 + 33 = ☐

STEP 3 (1.5 min) Challenge

Start the timer

Fill in the missing numbers.

☐ + 18 = 50   29 + ☐ = 61   90 – ☐ = 55

☐ + 23 = 41   ☐ – 22 = 30   82 – ☐ = 12

36 = 72 – ☐   82 = 29 + ☐   48 = ☐ – 27

Time spent: ________ min ________ sec. Total: ________ out of 35

28 Addition and subtraction of two-digit numbers (3)

Date: ______

Day of Week: ______

STEP 1 (1 min) Warm-up

Start the timer

Answer these.

25 + 50 = ☐ 29 − 20 = ☐ 39 + 5 = ☐ 27 + 36 = ☐

56 − 9 = ☐ 96 − 48 = ☐ 44 + 16 = ☐ 63 − 33 = ☐

STEP 2 (2.5 min) Rapid calculation

Start the timer

Answer these.

57 − 37 = ☐ 36 + 36 = ☐ 45 + 28 = ☐ 65 − 20 = ☐

34 + 48 = ☐ 70 − 25 = ☐ 27 + 59 = ☐ 84 − 56 = ☐

72 − 58 = ☐ 18 + 49 = ☐ 69 + 23 = ☐ 79 − 14 = ☐

63 − 49 = ☐ 90 − 47 = ☐ 39 + 49 = ☐ 58 + 25 = ☐

33 + 27 = ☐ 80 − 35 = ☐

STEP 3 (1.5 min) Challenge

Start the timer

Fill in the missing numbers.

☐ + 67 = 81 21 + ☐ = 40 94 − ☐ = 82

☐ − 24 = 75 85 − ☐ = 38 ☐ + 36 = 63

99 = ☐ + 31 + 5 63 = ☐ − 31 − 5 31 + ☐ = 99 − 63

Time spent: ______ min ______ sec. Total: ______ out of 35

Date: ______________________

Day of Week: ______________________

Addition and subtraction of two-digit numbers (4)

STEP 1 (1 min) Warm-up

Start the timer

Answer these.

22 + 28 = ☐ 27 + 33 = ☐ 32 + 38 = ☐ 37 + 43 = ☐

42 + 48 = ☐ 97 – 79 = ☐ 85 – 58 = ☐ 73 – 37 = ☐

STEP 2 (2.5 min) Rapid calculation

Start the timer

Answer these.

57 + 37 = ☐ 36 – 36 = ☐ 45 – 28 = ☐ 65 + 20 = ☐

95 – 48 = ☐ 70 + 25 = ☐ 57 – 19 = ☐ 27 + 56 = ☐

22 + 58 = ☐ 47 – 18 = ☐ 69 – 23 = ☐ 79 + 14 = ☐

63 + 19 = ☐ 50 + 47 = ☐ 87 – 48 = ☐ 58 – 25 = ☐

61 – 16 = ☐ 80 – 35 = ☐

STEP 3 (1.5 min) Challenge

Start the timer

Fill in the missing numbers.

☐ – 23 = 47 53 + ☐ = 90 83 – ☐ = 21

☐ – 73 = 19 86 – ☐ = 67 ☐ + 27 = 61

75 = ☐ + 23 + 22 37 = ☐ – 12 – 15 23 + ☐ = 46 – 23

Time spent: ________ min ________ sec. Total: ________ out of 35

30 Addition and subtraction of two-digit numbers (5)

Date:

Day of Week:

STEP 1 (1 min) Warm-up

Start the timer

Answer these.

£34 + £16 =	38p – 19p =
£18 + £22 =	65p – 38p =
£45 + £25 =	55p – 26p =
£17 + £53 =	72p – 33p =
£51 + £39 =	93p – 88p =

STEP 2 (2.5 min) Rapid calculation

Start the timer

Answer these.

24 m + 34 m =	56 m – 36 m =
75 m – 37 m =	63 m + 30 m =
84 cm – 36 cm =	50 cm + 25 cm =
33 cm – 18 cm =	48 cm + 27 cm =
54 m + 36 m =	45 m – 26 m =
69 m + 15 m =	35 m + 35 m =
74 cm + 17 cm =	38 cm + 40 cm =
86 cm – 29 cm =	98 cm – 77 cm =
46 cm + 19 cm =	73 cm – 18 cm =

STEP 3 (1.5 min) Challenge

Start the timer

Fill in the missing amounts.

☐ – £34 = £26   £45 + ☐ = £90   £66 – ☐ = £33

☐ – £54 = £18   £37 – ☐ = £19   ☐ + £44 = £82

97p = ☐ + 14p + 22p   55p = ☐ – 18p – 14p   33p + ☐ = 72p – 15p

Time spent: ________ min ________ sec. Total: ________ out of 37

Date: ______________________

Day of Week: ________________

Adding three numbers (1)

31

STEP 1 (1 min) Warm-up

Start the timer

Answer these.

3 + 5 + 5 = ☐   8 + 2 + 3 = ☐   1 + 4 + 6 = ☐   7 + 2 + 3 = ☐

3 + 9 + 1 = ☐   5 + 5 + 6 = ☐   8 + 5 + 2 = ☐   5 + 4 + 5 = ☐

STEP 2 (2.5 min) Rapid calculation

Start the timer

Answer these.

9 + 1 + 1 = ☐   8 + 2 + 2 = ☐   4 + 3 + 5 = ☐   3 + 1 + 7 = ☐

7 + 4 + 8 = ☐   7 + 5 + 6 = ☐   7 + 3 + 4 = ☐   1 + 9 + 5 = ☐

5 + 7 + 5 = ☐   4 + 8 + 6 = ☐   4 + 8 + 7 = ☐   3 + 8 + 6 = ☐

7 + 5 + 3 = ☐   3 + 7 + 8 = ☐   7 + 7 + 1 = ☐   6 + 6 + 4 = ☐

5 + 4 + 4 = ☐   3 + 3 + 6 = ☐

STEP 3 (1.5 min) Challenge

Start the timer

Answer these.

9 + 7 + 9 = ☐   8 + 8 + 9 = ☐

9 + 7 + 8 = ☐   7 + 7 + 6 = ☐

8 + 6 + 8 = ☐   9 + 9 + 9 = ☐

7 + 7 + 7 = ☐   8 + 8 + 8 = ☐

Time spent: ________ min ________ sec. Total: ________ out of 34

32 Adding three numbers (2)

Date: ______________

Day of Week: ______________

STEP 1 (1 min) Warm-up

Start the timer

Answer these.

5 + 7 = ☐	6 + 6 = ☐	8 + 4 = ☐	7 + 8 = ☐
12 + 4 = ☐	12 + 6 = ☐	6 + 6 + 8 = ☐	8 + 7 + 6 = ☐

STEP 2 (2.5 min) Rapid calculation

Start the timer

Answer these.

6 + 5 + 6 = ☐	7 + 7 + 6 = ☐	9 + 4 + 3 = ☐	8 + 4 + 5 = ☐
9 + 3 + 2 = ☐	6 + 8 + 8 = ☐	5 + 5 + 5 = ☐	8 + 2 + 8 = ☐
6 + 6 + 6 = ☐	6 + 0 + 9 = ☐	3 + 9 + 7 = ☐	9 + 9 + 9 = ☐
8 + 4 + 8 = ☐	7 + 8 + 6 = ☐	1 + 5 + 6 = ☐	2 + 3 + 7 = ☐
5 + 7 + 4 = ☐	3 + 3 + 3 = ☐		

STEP 3 (1.5 min) Challenge

Start the timer

Fill in the missing numbers.

☐ + 4 + 7 = 13	5 + ☐ + 1 = 12
6 + 5 + ☐ = 16	7 + ☐ + 3 = 19
☐ + 2 + 7 = 18	8 + 8 + ☐ = 21
7 + 4 + ☐ = 20	☐ + 9 + 9 = 18

Time spent: ________ min ________ sec. Total: ________ out of 34

Date: ____________________

Day of Week: ____________________

Adding three numbers (3)

STEP 1 (1 min) Warm-up

Start the timer

Answer these.

$3 + 8 = \square$ $5 + 5 = \square$ $9 + 6 = \square$ $8 + 7 = \square$

$11 + 7 = \square$ $10 + 8 = \square$ $9 + 6 + 6 = \square$ $7 + 8 + 9 = \square$

STEP 2 (2.5 min) Rapid calculation

Start the timer

Answer these.

$7 + 2 + 2 = \square$ $4 + 4 + 4 = \square$ $5 + 6 + 7 = \square$ $2 + 9 + 2 = \square$

$8 + 5 + 7 = \square$ $6 + 4 + 8 = \square$ $7 + 7 + 7 = \square$ $9 + 0 + 9 = \square$

$4 + 8 + 7 = \square$ $6 + 9 + 6 = \square$ $9 + 1 + 8 = \square$ $6 + 7 + 4 = \square$

$9 + 9 + 6 = \square$ $8 + 7 + 9 = \square$ $5 + 1 + 7 = \square$ $8 + 8 + 1 = \square$

$3 + 8 + 7 = \square$ $5 + 5 + 8 = \square$

STEP 3 (1.5 min) Challenge

Start the timer

Fill in the missing numbers.

$\square + 3 + 4 = 10$ $6 + \square + 2 = 15$

$7 + 4 + \square = 18$ $6 + \square + 6 = 12$

$\square + 9 + 5 = 16$ $6 + 6 + \square = 18$

$8 + 7 + \square = 19$ $\square + 8 + 8 = 20$

Time spent: ______ min ______ sec. Total: ______ out of 34

34 General review (1)

Date: ____________

Day of Week: ____________

STEP 1 (1 min) Warm-up

Start the timer

Answer these.

21 + 14 = ☐	63 + 25 = ☐	46 + 33 = ☐	64 + 23 = ☐
40 − 35 = ☐	85 − 23 = ☐	78 − 44 = ☐	21 + 19 = ☐

STEP 2 (2.5 min) Rapid calculation

Start the timer

Answer these.

44 + 28 = ☐	78 + 18 = ☐	62 − 35 = ☐	71 − 52 = ☐
72 − 28 = ☐	96 − 18 = ☐	27 + 35 = ☐	19 + 52 = ☐
54 − 28 = ☐	81 − 67 = ☐	61 − 44 = ☐	57 − 29 = ☐
83 − 79 = ☐	38 + 43 = ☐	42 − 19 = ☐	29 + 37 = ☐
63 + 28 = ☐	42 − 37 = ☐		

STEP 3 (1.5 min) Challenge

Start the timer

Fill in the missing numbers.

☐ + 18 = 40	29 + ☐ = 51	62 = 36 + ☐
☐ + 24 = 42	72 + ☐ = 100	29 = 82 − ☐
74 − ☐ = 58	☐ − 36 = 27	48 = ☐ − 27

Time spent: ______ min ______ sec. Total: ______ out of 35

Date: ____________________

Day of Week: ____________________

General review (2) 35

STEP 1 (1 min) Warm-up

Start the timer

Answer these.

39 + 15 = ☐ 48 + 26 = ☐ 76 + 22 = ☐ 57 + 34 = ☐

3 + 39 = ☐ 55 + 19 = ☐ 48 + 15 = ☐ 46 + 49 = ☐

STEP 2 (2.5 min) Rapid calculation

Start the timer

Fill in the missing numbers. The first one has been done for you.

39 + 17 = **40** + **16** = **56**

78 + 14 = ☐ + ☐ = ☐ 68 + 23 = ☐ + ☐ = ☐

43 + 28 = ☐ + ☐ = ☐ 66 + 26 = ☐ + ☐ = ☐

75 + 18 = ☐ + ☐ = ☐ 49 + 45 = ☐ + ☐ = ☐

57 + 16 = ☐ + ☐ = ☐ 38 + 36 = ☐ + ☐ = ☐

STEP 3 (1.5 min) Challenge

Start the timer

Answer these.

29 + 34 = ☐ 52 + 29 = ☐ 63 + 28 = ☐

47 + 35 = ☐ 35 + 57 = ☐ 32 + 49 = ☐

77 + 18 = ☐ 19 + 29 = ☐ 58 + 19 = ☐

42 + 29 = ☐ 18 + 37 = ☐ 39 + 44 = ☐

Time spent: ______ min ______ sec. Total: ______ out of 28

36 General review (3)

Date: ____________

Day of Week: ____________

STEP 1 (1 min) Warm-up

Start the timer

Answer these.

62 – 28 = ☐ 72 – 15 = ☐ 55 – 38 = ☐ 91 – 46 = ☐

82 – 61 = ☐ 82 – 54 = ☐ 83 – 39 = ☐ 56 – 37 = ☐

STEP 2 (2.5 min) Rapid calculation

Start the timer

Fill in the missing numbers. The first one has been done for you.

52 – 16 = **50** – **14** = **36**

81 – 29 = ☐ – ☐ = ☐ 81 – 28 = ☐ – ☐ = ☐

81 – 26 = ☐ – ☐ = ☐ 66 – 19 = ☐ – ☐ = ☐

66 – 18 = ☐ – ☐ = ☐ 66 – 17 = ☐ – ☐ = ☐

91 – 23 = ☐ – ☐ = ☐ 72 – 27 = ☐ – ☐ = ☐

STEP 3 (1.5 min) Challenge

Start the timer

Answer these.

36 – 29 = ☐ 57 – 38 = ☐ 62 – 34 = ☐

84 – 35 = ☐ 91 – 47 = ☐ 75 – 59 = ☐

43 – 24 = ☐ 53 – 28 = ☐ 68 – 39 = ☐

74 – 27 = ☐ 66 – 38 = ☐ 36 – 19 = ☐

Time spent: ______ min ______ sec. Total: ______ out of 28

Date: ____________________

Day of Week: ____________________

STEP 1 (1 min) Warm-up

Start the timer

Answer these.

37 + 24 = ☐ 63 + 27 = ☐ 44 + 38 = ☐ 29 + 42 = ☐

66 − 27 = ☐ 41 − 22 = ☐ 74 − 58 = ☐ 45 − 29 = ☐

STEP 2 (2.5 min) Rapid calculation

Start the timer

Fill in the missing numbers. The first one has been done for you.

25 + 25 = **30** + **20** = **50**

46 + 46 = ☐ + ☐ = ☐ 37 + 48 = ☐ + ☐ = ☐

24 + 67 = ☐ + ☐ = ☐ 52 + 17 = ☐ + ☐ = ☐

72 − 23 = ☐ − ☐ = ☐ 64 − 27 = ☐ − ☐ = ☐

82 − 57 = ☐ − ☐ = ☐ 91 − 38 = ☐ − ☐ = ☐

STEP 3 (1.5 min) Challenge

Start the timer

Answer these.

86 − 48 = ☐ 44 + 17 = ☐ 76 − 37 = ☐ 59 + 28 = ☐

97 − 38 = ☐ 83 − 36 = ☐ 44 + 29 = ☐ 68 + 14 = ☐

73 − 55 = ☐ 57 + 36 = ☐ 56 − 29 = ☐ 27 + 26 = ☐

Time spent: ________ min ________ sec. Total: ________ out of 28

38 General review (5)

Date: ______________________

Day of Week: ______________________

STEP 1 (1 min) Warm-up

Start the timer

Answer these.

24 + 38 = ☐	55 – 29 = ☐	46 + 39 = ☐	56 – 48 = ☐
80 – 46 = ☐	91 – 58 = ☐	26 + 39 = ☐	65 – 26 = ☐

STEP 2 (2.5 min) Rapid calculation

Start the timer

Fill in the missing numbers.

16 + ☐ = 47	☐ + 26 = 75	☐ + 27 = 55	☐ + 37 = 76
14 + ☐ = 68	56 + ☐ = 71	56 + ☐ = 83	☐ + 25 = 72
15 + ☐ = 53	☐ + 23 = 48	21 + ☐ = 50	☐ + 36 = 84
25 + ☐ = 91	38 + ☐ = 97	☐ + 52 = 86	☐ + 44 = 80

STEP 3 (1.5 min) Challenge

Start the timer

Fill in each box with **>**, **<** or **=**.

8 + 7 + 5 ☐ 34 – 13	3 + 9 + 6 ☐ 44 – 27
4 + 8 + 9 ☐ 9 + 12	6 + 9 + 9 ☐ 43 – 20
8 + 6 + 7 ☐ 84 – 62	8 + 8 + 7 ☐ 92 – 69
8 + 9 + 9 ☐ 9 + 16	9 + 9 + 9 ☐ 15 + 13

Time spent: ________ min ________ sec. Total: ________ out of 32

Date: ____________________

Day of Week: ____________________

General review (6) 39

STEP 1 (1 min) Warm-up

Start the timer

Answer these.

4 + 3 + 6 = ☐ 9 + 5 + 3 = ☐ 5 + 7 + 2 = ☐ 3 + 8 + 7 = ☐

6 + 7 + 9 = ☐ 9 + 9 + 7 = ☐ 7 + 8 + 8 = ☐ 7 + 6 + 7 = ☐

STEP 2 (2.5 min) Rapid calculation

Start the timer

Fill in each box with **>**, **<** or **=**.

8 + 9 + 8 ☐ 33 – 9

5 + 4 + 7 ☐ 45 – 28

7 + 4 + 8 ☐ 53 – 34

8 + 7 + 9 ☐ 62 – 38

9 + 9 + 8 ☐ 43 – 16

9 + 5 + 7 ☐ 85 – 65

8 + 8 + 8 ☐ 81 – 57

9 + 9 + 9 ☐ 95 – 67

6 + 6 + 7 ☐ 75 – 55

5 + 8 + 4 ☐ 31 – 15

STEP 3 (1.5 min) Challenge

Start the timer

Fill in the missing numbers.

95 – ☐ = 27 + 14

☐ – 35 = 78 – 21

☐ – 31 = 27 + 19

71 – ☐ = 73 – 25

66 – ☐ = 33 + 18

☐ – 27 = 43 – 17

83 – ☐ = 63 – 13

☐ – 37 = 26 + 31

Time spent: ________ min ________ sec. Total: ________ out of 26

40 General review (7)

Date: ____________________

Day of Week: ____________________

STEP 1 (1 min) Warm-up

Start the timer

Answer these.

£5 + £7 + £9 = ☐   £7 + £6 + £5 = ☐   £3 + £5 + £7 = ☐

£2 + £8 + £8 = ☐   4p + 4p + 5p = ☐   6p + 7p + 7p = ☐

9p + 4p + 5p = ☐   8p + 5p + 4p = ☐

STEP 2 (2.5 min) Rapid calculation

Start the timer

Fill in each box with **>**, **<** or **=**.

10 m + 6 m + 6 m ☐ 41 m – 20 m   7 m + 10 m + 7 m ☐ 53 m – 28 m

8 m + 5 m + 10 m ☐ 67 m – 45 m   5 cm + 10 cm + 9 cm ☐ 62 cm – 37 cm

10 cm + 8 cm + 8 cm ☐ 91 cm – 65 cm   9 cm + 9 cm + 10 cm ☐ 85 cm – 58 cm

9 m + 5 m + 9 m ☐ 81 m – 58 m   6 cm + 8 cm + 3 cm ☐ 99 cm – 81 cm

STEP 3 (1.5 min) Challenge

Start the timer

Fill in the missing amounts.

£95 – ☐ = £32 + £16   ☐ – £35 = £54 – £21

☐ – £31 = £19 + £45   £71 – ☐ = £65 – £23

66p – ☐ = 12p + 35p   ☐ – 27p = 58p – 14p

83p – ☐ = 92p – 61p   ☐ – 37p = 18p + 28p

Time spent: ________ min ________ sec. Total: ________ out of 24

Date: ____________

Day of Week: ____________

General review (8) 41

STEP 1 (1 min) Warm-up

Start the timer

A car journey is completed in two stages. What is the total distance travelled in each journey?

26 km and 45 km Total: ☐ km

34 km and 38 km Total: ☐ km

45 km and 29 km Total: ☐ km

53 km and 19 km Total: ☐ km

65 km and 28 km Total: ☐ km

47 km and 47 km Total: ☐ km

STEP 2 (2.5 min) Rapid calculation

Start the timer

The money in three piggy banks is added together. What is the total amount in each piggy bank?

£5, £7 and £8 Total: £ ☐

£8, £6 and £4 Total: £ ☐

£3, £7 and £10 Total: £ ☐

£9, £5 and £6 Total: £ ☐

£10, £8 and £8 Total: £ ☐

£9, £10 and £9 Total: £ ☐

£6, £9 and £9 Total: £ ☐

£4, £8 and £7 Total: £ ☐

£6, £6 and £5 Total: £ ☐

£3, £10 and £9 Total: £ ☐

STEP 3 (1.5 min) Challenge

Start the timer

Fill in the missing numbers.

1. Harry has £37. He wants to save £74. How much more money does he need? £ ☐

2. Leona has £44. She wants to save £92. How much more money does she need? £ ☐

3. Faisal has £59. He wants to save £97. How much more money does he need? £ ☐

4. Lara has £18. She wants to save £85. How much more money does she need? £ ☐

Time spent: ______ min ______ sec. Total: ______ out of 20

42 Commutative law of addition (1)

Date: ______

Day of Week: ______

STEP 1 (1 min) Warm-up

Start the timer

Answer these.

37 + 48 = ☐	48 + 37 = ☐	68 + 27 = ☐	27 + 68 = ☐
73 + 19 = ☐	19 + 73 = ☐	45 + 47 = ☐	47 + 45 = ☐
39 + 55 = ☐	55 + 39 = ☐	49 + 37 = ☐	37 + 49 = ☐

STEP 2 (2.5 min) Rapid calculation

Start the timer

Fill in the missing numbers.

1. 25 + 34 = 34 + ☐ = ☐
2. 67 + 16 = ☐ + 67 = ☐
3. 58 + 37 = 37 + ☐ = ☐
4. 47 + 25 = 25 + ☐ = ☐
5. 59 + 24 = ☐ + 59 = ☐
6. 29 + 47 = 47 + ☐ = ☐
7. 23 + 68 = ☐ + ☐ = ☐
8. 75 + 18 = ☐ + ☐ = ☐
9. 43 + 35 = ☐ + ☐ = ☐
10. 18 + 68 = ☐ + ☐ = ☐
11. 83 + 16 = ☐ + ☐ = ☐
12. 37 + 44 = ☐ + ☐ = ☐

STEP 3 (1.5 min) Challenge

Start the timer

Fill in the missing numbers row by row.

1. 57 + 26 = ☐	56 + 27 = ☐	54 + 29 = ☐	52 + 31 = ☐
2. 37 + 49 = ☐	39 + 47 = ☐	33 + 53 = ☐	☐ + 59 = ☐
3. 76 + 22 = ☐	66 + 32 = ☐	52 + 46 = ☐	40 + ☐ = ☐
4. 52 + 39 = ☐	☐ + 49 = ☐	☐ + ☐ = ☐	☐ + ☐ = ☐

Time spent: ______ min ______ sec. Total: ______ out of 40

Date: ____________________

Day of Week: ____________________

STEP 1 (1 min) Warm-up

Start the timer

Fill in the missing numbers.

35 + 46 = 46 + ☐ = ☐

57 + 36 = 36 + ☐ = ☐

29 + 58 = ☐ + ☐ = ☐

78 + 14 = ☐ + ☐ = ☐

67 + 28 = ☐ + ☐ = ☐

26 + 49 = ☐ + ☐ = ☐

STEP 2 (2.5 min) Rapid calculation

Start the timer

Fill in the missing numbers.

1. 36 + 47 = ☐ + 36 = ☐ + 46 = 33 + ☐ = ☐
2. 29 + 56 = 56 + ☐ = 26 + ☐ = ☐ + 55 = ☐
3. 51 + 38 = ☐ + 58 = 61 + ☐ = ☐ + 40 = ☐
4. 32 + 54 = ☐ + 52 = 30 + ☐ = ☐ + 60 = ☐
5. 53 + 45 = ☐ + 50 = 60 + ☐ = ☐ + 40 = ☐
6. 66 + 23 = 60 + ☐ = 70 + ☐ = ☐ + 30 = ☐
7. 24 + 52 = 30 + ☐ = ☐ + 60 = ☐ + 56 = ☐
8. 29 + 55 = ☐ + 54 = 24 + ☐ = ☐ + 50 = ☐

STEP 3 (1.5 min) Challenge

Start the timer

Fill in the missing numbers row by row.

1. 35 + 51 = ☐ 30 + 56 = ☐ 40 + 46 = ☐ ☐ + ☐ = ☐
2. 48 + 30 = ☐ 40 + 38 = ☐ 50 + 28 = ☐ ☐ + ☐ = ☐
3. 63 + 28 = ☐ 68 + 23 = ☐ 60 + 31 = ☐ ☐ + ☐ = ☐
4. 76 + 21 = ☐ 71 + 26 = ☐ 80 + 17 = ☐ ☐ + ☐ = ☐

Time spent: ______ min ______ sec. Total: ______ out of 30

44 Odd and even numbers

Date: ______________________

Day of Week: ______________________

STEP 1 (1 min) Warm-up

Start the timer

1. Circle the odd numbers.

13	44	21	12	36	46	8	35	47	54
49	50	38	34	22	85	79	57	68	90

2. Circle the even numbers.

88	37	46	21	89	54	42	92	98	65
34	53	64	74	67	70	31	2	23	100

STEP 2 (2.5 min) Rapid calculation

Start the timer

1. Write all the odd numbers between:

4 and 10 ______________________ 14 and 20 ______________________

32 and 38 ______________________ 50 and 60 ______________________

75 and 85 ______________________ 83 and 93 ______________________

2. Write all the even numbers between:

1 and 7 ______________________ 13 and 19 ______________________

24 and 30 ______________________ 40 and 50 ______________________

64 and 74 ______________________ 88 and 98 ______________________

STEP 3 (1.5 min) Challenge

Start the timer

1. 45 78 24 82 47 64 27 44 20 76 65 51

Greatest even number = ☐ Smallest odd number = ☐

2. 34 53 10 87 68 75 17 33 59 73 24 35

Greatest even number = ☐ Smallest odd number = ☐

3. 23 15 67 34 71 59 75 64 31 87 57 85

Greatest even number = ☐ Smallest odd number = ☐

4. 61 77 43 87 49 71 80 73 40 74 97 48

Greatest even number = ☐ Smallest odd number = ☐

Time spent: ________ min ________ sec. Total: ________ out of 40

Date: ____________

Day of Week: ____________

Introduction to multiplication (1)

STEP 1 (1 min) Warm-up

Start the timer

Answer these.

2 + 2 + 2 = ☐	3 + 3 + 3 = ☐	4 + 4 + 4 + 4 = ☐	5 + 5 + 5 + 5 = ☐
6 + 6 + 6 = ☐	7 + 7 + 7 = ☐	3 + 3 + 3 + 3 = ☐	6 + 6 + 6 + 6 = ☐
4 + 4 + 4 = ☐	9 + 9 + 9 = ☐	7 + 7 + 7 + 7 = ☐	8 + 8 + 8 + 8 + 8 = ☐

STEP 2 (2.5 min) Rapid calculation

Start the timer

Fill in the missing numbers.

2 + 2 + 2 + 2 = ☐ × 2 = ☐	4 + 4 + 4 = ☐ × 4 = ☐
3 + 3 + 3 + 3 = ☐ × 3 = ☐	1 + 1 + 1 + 1 + 1 = ☐ × 1 = ☐
5 + 5 + 5 + 5 = ☐ × 5 = ☐	7 + 7 + 7 = ☐ × 7 = ☐
9 + 9 + 9 = ☐ × 9 = ☐	8 + 8 + 8 + 8 = ☐ × 8 = ☐
6 + 6 + 6 + 6 + 6 = ☐ × ☐ = ☐	7 + 7 + 7 + 7 + 7 = ☐ × ☐ = ☐
1 + 1 + 1 + 1 + 1 + 1 + 1 = ☐ × ☐ = ☐	3 + 3 + 3 = ☐ × ☐ = ☐
5 + 5 + 5 + 5 + 5 + 5 + 5 + 5 = ☐ × ☐ = ☐	8 + 8 = ☐ × ☐ = ☐

STEP 3 (1.5 min) Challenge

Start the timer

Fill in the missing numbers.

3 + 3 + 3 + 3 + 3 + 3 + 3 + 3 + 3 = ☐ × ☐ = ☐

8 + 8 + 8 + 8 + 8 + 8 + 8 = ☐ × ☐ = ☐

10 + 10 + 10 + 10 = ☐ × ☐ = ☐

9 + 9 + 9 + 9 + 9 + 9 + 9 + 9 = ☐ × ☐ = ☐

12 + 12 + 12 + 12 + 12 + 12 + 12 + 12 = ☐ × ☐ = ☐

Time spent: ______ min ______ sec. Total: ______ out of 31

46 Introduction to multiplication (2)

Date: ____________________

Day of Week: ____________________

STEP 1 (1 min) Warm-up

Start the timer

Answer these.

1 × 1 = ☐ 2 × 2 = ☐ 3 × 3 = ☐ 4 × 4 = ☐

5 × 5 = ☐ 5 × 0 = ☐ 3 × 2 = ☐ 4 × 1 = ☐

STEP 2 (2.5 min) Rapid calculation

Start the timer

Fill in the boxes. Some have been done for you.

1. 2 + 2 + 2 + 2 + 2 + 2 = **6** × **2** = ☐ 6 × 2 = **2** × **6** = ☐

2. 3 + 3 + 3 + 3 = ☐ × ☐ = ☐ 4 × 3 = ☐ × **4** = ☐

3. 1 + 1 + 1 + 1 + 1 = ☐ × ☐ = ☐ 5 × 1 = ☐ × ☐ = ☐

4. 4 + 4 + 4 + 4 + 4 = ☐ × ☐ = ☐ 5 × 4 = ☐ × ☐ = ☐

5. 5 + 5 + 5 = ☐ × ☐ = ☐ 3 × 5 = ☐ × ☐ = ☐

6. 6 + 6 + 6 + 6 = ☐ × ☐ = ☐ 4 × 6 = ☐ × ☐ = ☐

7. 7 + 7 + 7 + 7 = ☐ × ☐ = ☐ 4 × 7 = ☐ × ☐ = ☐

STEP 3 (1.5 min) Challenge

Start the timer

Fill in the boxes. Some have been done for you.

1. 3 × 4 = **4** + **4** + **4** = ☐ 4 × 3 = ☐ + ☐ + ☐ + ☐ = ☐

2. 5 × 2 = ☐ + ☐ + ☐ + ☐ + ☐ = ☐ 2 × 5 = ☐ + ☐ = ☐

3. 4 × 6 = ☐ + ☐ + ☐ + ☐ = ☐

6 × 4 = ☐ + ☐ + ☐ + ☐ + ☐ + ☐ = ☐

Time spent: ________ min ________ sec. Total: ________ out of 28

Date: ____________________

Day of Week: ____________________

STEP 1 (1 min) Warm-up

Start the timer

Answer these.

$2 + 2 + 2 =$ ☐

$10 + 10 + 10 + 10 =$ ☐

$10 + 10 + 10 =$ ☐

$10 + 10 + 10 + 10 + 10 =$ ☐

$5 + 5 + 5 + 5 + 5 + 5 =$ ☐

$5 + 5 + 5 + 5 =$ ☐

$5 + 5 + 5 =$ ☐

$2 + 2 + 2 + 2 =$ ☐

$2 + 2 + 2 + 2 + 2 + 2 =$ ☐

$10 + 10 + 10 + 10 + 10 + 10 + 10 =$ ☐

STEP 2 (2.5 min) Rapid calculation

Start the timer

Complete the table. The first row has been done for you.

5 + 5 = 10	**two 5s**	**2 times 5**	**2 × 5 = 10**
2 + 2 + 2 + 2 + 2 = 10			
10 + 10 + 10 + 10 = 40			
2 + 2 + 2 + 2 + 2 + 2 + 2 + 2 = 16			
10 + 10 + 10 + 10 + 10 + 10 = 60			
5 + 5 + 5 + 5 + 5 = 25			

STEP 3 (1.5 min) Challenge

Start the timer

Complete the table. The first row has been done for you.

2 + 2 + 2 + 2 = **8**	**4 × 2 = 8**	**2 × 4 = 8**
5 + 5 =		
10 + 10 + 10 =		
2 + 2 + 2 + 2 + 2 =		
5 + 5 + 5 + 5 + 5 + 5 + 5 =		
10 + 10 + 10 + 10 + 10 + 10 + 10 =		
5 + 5 + 5 + 5 + 5 + 5 + 5 + 5 =		
2 + 2 + 2 + 2 + 2 + 2 + 2 + 2 + 2 + 2 =		

Time spent: ________ min ________ sec. Total: ________ out of 46

48 Times (2)

Date: ______________________

Day of Week: ______________________

STEP 1 (1 min) Warm-up

Start the timer

Answer these.

10 + 10 + 10 + 10 + 10 + 10 + 10 + 10 = ☐

5 + 5 + 5 + 5 + 5 + 5 + 5 + 5 = ☐

10 + 10 + 10 + 10 + 10 + 10 + 10 + 10 + 10 = ☐

2 + 2 + 2 + 2 + 2 + 2 + 2 = ☐

2 + 2 + 2 + 2 + 2 + 2 + 2 + 2 = ☐

5 + 5 + 5 + 5 + 5 + 5 + 5 + 5 + 5 + 5 = ☐

STEP 2 (2.5 min) Rapid calculation

Start the timer

Complete the table. The first row has been done for you.

10 + 10 + 10 + 10 + 10 + 10 + 10 = 70	**seven 10s**	**7 times 10**	**7 × 10 = 70**
5 + 5 + 5 + 5 + 5 + 5 + 5 + 5 + 5 = 45			
2 + 2 + 2 + 2 + 2 + 2 + 2 + 2 + 2 = 18			
5 + 5 + 5 + 5 + 5 + 5 + 5 = 35			
2 + 2 + 2 + 2 + 2 + 2 + 2 + 2 + 2 + 2 = 20			
10 + 10 + 10 + 10 + 10 + 10 + 10 + 10 + 10 = 90			

STEP 3 (1.5 min) Challenge

Start the timer

Complete the table. The first row has been done for you.

2 + 2 + 2 + 2 + 2 + 2 = **12**	**6 × 2 = 12**	**2 × 6 = 12**
5 + 5 + 5 + 5 + 5 + 5 + 5 + 5 =		
10 + 10 + 10 + 10 + 10 + 10 + 10 + 10 =		
2 + 2 + 2 + 2 + 2 + 2 + 2 =		
10 + 10 + 10 + 10 + 10 + 10 + 10 + 10 + 10 + 10 =		
5 + 5 + 5 + 5 + 5 + 5 + 5 + 5 + 5 + 5 =		
2 + 2 + 2 + 2 + 2 + 2 + 2 + 2 + 2 =		

Time spent: ________ min ________ sec. Total: ________ out of 39

Date: ____________________

Day of Week: ____________________

Multiplication as an array

STEP 1 (1 min) Warm-up

Start the timer

Complete the table. The first row has been done for you.

Array	Number of rows	Number of columns	Total number of dots
●●● ●●●	2	3	6
●●●●● ●●●●● ●●●●●			
●●●●●●●●●● ●●●●●●●●●●			
●●●●● ●●●●●			
●●●● ●●●● ●●●● ●●●● ●●●●			
●●●●● ●●●●● ●●●●● ●●●●● ●●●●● ●●●●● ●●●●● ●●●●● ●●●●● ●●●●●			

STEP 2 (2.5 min) Rapid calculation

Start the timer

Complete two multiplications for each array. The first one has been done for you.

●●●● ●●●●	●●●●● ●●●●●	●●●●●●●●●● ●●●●●●●●●● ●●●●●●●●●●	●●●●●●● ●●●●●●●	●●●●● ●●●●● ●●●●● ●●●●●	●●●●●●●●●● ●●●●●●●●●● ●●●●●●●●●● ●●●●●●●●●● ●●●●●●●●●●
2 × 4 = 8					
4 × 2 = 8					

STEP 3 (1.5 min) Challenge

Start the timer

How many coins are there in:

4 rows of 2 coins? ☐

6 rows of 5 coins? ☐

7 rows of 10 coins? ☐

2 rows of 9 coins? ☐

8 rows of 5 coins? ☐

9 rows of 10 coins? ☐

Time spent: ________ min ________ sec. Total: ________ out of 31

50 Multiplication of 10 (1)

Date: ____________________

Day of Week: ____________________

STEP 1 (1 min) Warm-up

Start the timer

Answer these.

10 + 10 = ☐	80 − 10 = ☐	60 − 10 = ☐	90 − 10 = ☐
10 + 40 = ☐	50 + 10 = ☐	10 + 60 = ☐	10 + 70 = ☐
10 + 10 + 10 = ☐	10 + 0 + 10 = ☐	10 + 10 + 10 + 10 = ☐	

STEP 2 (2.5 min) Rapid calculation

Start the timer

Answer these.

1 × 10 = ☐	2 × 10 = ☐	3 × 10 = ☐	4 × 10 = ☐
5 × 10 = ☐	6 × 10 = ☐	7 × 10 = ☐	8 × 10 = ☐
9 × 10 = ☐	10 × 10 = ☐	10 × 1 = ☐	10 × 2 = ☐
10 × 3 = ☐	10 × 4 = ☐	10 × 5 = ☐	10 × 6 = ☐
10 × 11 = ☐	10 × 8 = ☐	10 × 12 = ☐	10 × 0 = ☐

STEP 3 (1.5 min) Challenge

Start the timer

TIP *In a mathematical sentence with mixed multiplication and addition, or multiplication and subtraction, do the multiplication first.*

Answer these.

3 × 10 + 2 = ☐	5 × 10 + 5 = ☐	10 × 9 + 9 = ☐
10 × 7 + 6 = ☐	6 × 10 + 8 = ☐	12 × 10 − 9 = ☐
11 × 10 + 6 = ☐	10 × 10 − 10 = ☐	8 + 10 × 4 = ☐

Time spent: ________ min ________ sec. Total: ________ out of 40

Date: ____________________

Day of Week: ____________________

Multiplication of 10 (2)

STEP 1 (1 min) Warm-up

Start the timer

Answer these.

30 + 10 = ☐	70 − 10 = ☐	40 + 10 = ☐	20 + 10 = ☐
10 − 10 = ☐	50 − 10 = ☐	30 − 10 = ☐	80 + 10 = ☐
10 + 10 + 5 + 5 = ☐	20 − 5 − 5 = ☐	5 + 10 + 15 = ☐	

STEP 2 (2.5 min) Rapid calculation

Start the timer

Answer these.

4 × 10 = ☐	10 × 6 = ☐	10 × 4 = ☐	8 × 10 = ☐
10 × 9 = ☐	7 × 10 = ☐	2 × 10 = ☐	0 × 10 = ☐
10 × 1 = ☐	3 × 10 = ☐	10 × 11 = ☐	1 × 10 = ☐
12 × 10 = ☐	10 × 2 = ☐	5 × 10 = ☐	10 × 7 = ☐
6 × 10 = ☐	10 × 3 = ☐	10 × 10 = ☐	10 × 5 = ☐

STEP 3 (1.5 min) Challenge

Start the timer

Answer these.

5 × 10 + 24 = ☐	4 × 10 − 15 = ☐	10 × 2 + 37 = ☐
10 × 4 + 59 = ☐	8 × 10 − 35 = ☐	10 × 10 − 36 = ☐
1 × 10 + 86 = ☐	5 × 10 + 27 = ☐	88 − 10 × 4 = ☐

Time spent: ______ min ______ sec. Total: ______ out of 40

52 Multiplication of 5 (1)

Date: ____________

Day of Week: ____________

STEP 1 (1 min) Warm-up

Start the timer

Answer these.

4 × 10 = ☐ 5 + 25 = ☐ 10 × 8 = ☐ 60 − 5 = ☐

10 × 10 = ☐ 7 × 10 = ☐ 40 − 5 = ☐ 20 + 5 = ☐

5 + 5 + 5 = ☐ 5 + 5 = ☐

STEP 2 (2.5 min) Rapid calculation

Start the timer

Answer these.

1 × 5 = ☐ 2 × 5 = ☐ 3 × 5 = ☐ 4 × 5 = ☐

5 × 5 = ☐ 6 × 5 = ☐ 7 × 5 = ☐ 8 × 5 = ☐

9 × 5 = ☐ 5 × 10 = ☐ 5 × 1 = ☐ 5 × 2 = ☐

5 × 3 = ☐ 5 × 4 = ☐ 5 × 0 = ☐ 5 × 7 = ☐

5 × 11 = ☐ 5 × 8 = ☐ 5 × 9 = ☐ 12 × 5 = ☐

STEP 3 (1.5 min) Challenge

Start the timer

Answer these.

5 × 10 = ☐ 4 × 5 = ☐ 5 × 2 = ☐ 5 × 4 = ☐

11 × 10 = ☐ 10 × 10 = ☐ 8 × 5 = ☐ 5 × 0 = ☐

8 × 10 = ☐ 0 × 10 = ☐ 0 × 5 = ☐ 9 × 5 = ☐

Time spent: ______ min ______ sec. Total: ______ out of 42

Date: ____________________

Day of Week: ____________________

Multiplication of 5 (2)

STEP 1 (1 min) Warm-up

Start the timer

Answer these.

5 + 40 = ☐	10 – 5 = ☐	8 × 10 = ☐	35 + 5 = ☐
10 × 7 = ☐	7 × 5 = ☐	55 – 5 = ☐	10 × 10 = ☐
50 – 5 = ☐	5 × 11 = ☐		

STEP 2 (2.5 min) Rapid calculation

Start the timer

Answer these.

4 × 5 = ☐	5 × 6 = ☐	5 × 5 = ☐	5 × 8 = ☐
5 × 12 = ☐	9 × 5 = ☐	5 × 7 = ☐	8 × 5 = ☐
11 × 5 = ☐	5 × 10 = ☐	5 × 1 = ☐	5 × 2 = ☐
5 × 9 = ☐	10 × 5 = ☐	1 × 5 = ☐	2 × 5 = ☐
12 × 5 = ☐	3 × 5 = ☐	6 × 5 = ☐	0 × 5 = ☐

STEP 3 (1.5 min) Challenge

Start the timer

Answer these.

5 × 5 + 2 = ☐	6 × 5 + 3 = ☐	5 + 5 × 2 = ☐
5 × 4 – 9 = ☐	5 × 4 – 3 = ☐	5 × 12 – 17 = ☐
62 – 11 × 5 = ☐	5 – 5 × 0 = ☐	3 × 5 + 29 = ☐
5 × 7 – 16 = ☐	2 × 5 + 90 = ☐	55 – 9 × 5 = ☐

Time spent: ________ min ________ sec. Total: ________ out of 42

54 Multiplication of 10 and 5 (1)

Date: ______________

Day of Week: ______________

STEP 1 (1 min) Warm-up

Start the timer

Answer these.

30 + 25 = ☐ 45 – 20 = ☐ 35 + 60 = ☐ 15 + 60 = ☐

65 – 45 = ☐ 55 – 35 = ☐ 25 + 60 = ☐ 70 – 15 = ☐

30 + 10 = ☐ 60 – 5 = ☐ 25 + 25 = ☐ 100 – 35 = ☐

STEP 2 (2.5 min) Rapid calculation

Start the timer

Fill in the missing numbers.

10 × 4 = ☐ 12 × 5 = ☐ 3 × 5 = ☐ 10 × 8 = ☐

7 × 5 = ☐ 9 × 10 = ☐ 5 × 6 = ☐ 10 × 11 = ☐

8 × 5 = ☐ 5 × 3 = ☐ 5 × 10 = ☐ 5 × 5 = ☐

10 × 9 = ☐ 1 × 5 = ☐ 9 × 5 = ☐ 10 × 0 = ☐

5 × ☐ = 45 ☐ × 10 = 120 5 × ☐ = 55 ☐ × 10 = 40

STEP 3 (1.5 min) Challenge

Start the timer

Fill in the missing numbers.

10 × 11 – 7 = ☐ 10 × 5 + 33 = ☐ 6 × 5 + 11 = ☐

5 × 12 – 12 = ☐ 8 × 5 + 24 = ☐ 0 × 10 + 10 = ☐

☐ – 4 × 5 = 15 45 – 5 × ☐ = 35 5 × 12 + ☐ = 100

Time spent: ______ min ______ sec. Total: ______ out of 41

Date: ______________________

Day of Week: ______________________

STEP 1 (1 min) Warm-up

Start the timer

Answer these.

55 – 30 = ☐ 70 – 35 = ☐ 20 + 20 = ☐ 30 + 30 = ☐

100 – 35 = ☐ 65 – 20 = ☐ 40 + 20 = ☐ 35 + 55 = ☐

60 + 25 = ☐ 90 – 35 = ☐ 80 + 15 = ☐ 100 – 75 = ☐

STEP 2 (2.5 min) Rapid calculation

Start the timer

Fill in the missing numbers.

5 × 7 = ☐ 3 × 5 = ☐ 8 × 5 = ☐ 5 × 2 = ☐

10 × 11 = ☐ 3 × 10 = ☐ 8 × 10 = ☐ 10 × 2 = ☐

10 × 5 = ☐ 10 × 4 = ☐ 12 × 10 = ☐ 9 × 10 = ☐

5 × 5 = ☐ 5 × 11 = ☐ 6 × 5 = ☐ 12 × 5 = ☐

5 × ☐ = 0 ☐ × 10 = 10 5 × ☐ = 50 ☐ × 10 = 100

STEP 3 (1.5 min) Challenge

Start the timer

Fill in the missing numbers.

10 × 7 – 9 = ☐ 10 × 4 + 57 = ☐ 6 × 10 – 11 = ☐

5 × 11 – 12 = ☐ 9 × 5 + 26 = ☐ 78 – 0 × 5 = ☐

☐ – 12 × 5 = 20 68 – 10 × ☐ = 68 5 × 10 + ☐ = 100

Time spent: ______ min ______ sec. Total: ______ out of 41

56 Multiplication of 2 (1)

Date: ______________________

Day of Week: ______________________

STEP 1 (1 min) Warm-up

Start the timer

Answer these.

$0 \times 2 = \square$ $10 - 2 = \square$ $4 \times 2 = \square$ $11 \times 2 = \square$

$5 + 5 = \square$ $2 \times 2 = \square$ $16 - 2 = \square$ $7 + 7 = \square$

$2 + 2 + 2 = \square$ $2 + 2 + 2 + 2 = \square$ $22 + 2 = \square$

STEP 2 (2.5 min) Rapid calculation

Start the timer

Answer these.

$2 \times 4 = \square$ $2 \times 5 = \square$ $3 \times 2 = \square$ $2 \times 8 = \square$

$2 \times 6 = \square$ $9 \times 2 = \square$ $6 \times 2 = \square$ $10 \times 2 = \square$

$8 \times 2 = \square$ $2 \times 3 = \square$ $2 \times 9 = \square$ $2 \times 7 = \square$

$7 \times 2 = \square$ $1 \times 2 = \square$ $12 \times 2 = \square$ $2 \times 0 = \square$

$5 \times 2 = \square$ $2 \times 10 = \square$ $2 \times 11 = \square$ $2 \times 1 = \square$

STEP 3 (1.5 min) Challenge

Start the timer

Fill in the missing numbers.

$\square \times 7 = 14$ $10 \times \square = 30$ $\square \times 2 = 16$

$4 \times \square = 8$ $2 \times \square = 24$ $\square \times 5 = 15$

$\square \times 11 = 22$ $\square \times 10 = 110$ $12 \times \square = 60$

Time spent: ________ min ________ sec. Total: ________ out of 40

Date: ____________________

Day of Week: ____________________

Multiplication of 2 (2)

57

STEP 1 (1 min) Warm-up

Start the timer

Answer these.

$2 \times 2 = \square$ $5 \times 2 = \square$ $6 \times 5 = \square$ $12 + 2 = \square$

$10 + 10 = \square$ $4 + 4 = \square$ $0 \times 2 = \square$ $20 - 2 = \square$

$8 - 2 - 2 = \square$ $12 - 2 - 2 = \square$ $20 - 2 - 2 = \square$

STEP 2 (2.5 min) Rapid calculation

Start the timer

Fill in the missing numbers.

$2 \times 6 = \square$ $7 \times 2 = \square$ $12 + 12 = \square$ $2 \times 4 = \square$

$9 + 9 = \square$ $6 \times 2 = \square$ $10 \times 2 = \square$ $1 \times 2 = \square$

$12 \times 2 = \square$ $8 + 8 = \square$ $3 + 3 = \square$ $9 \times 2 = \square$

$2 \times 5 = \square$ $11 + 11 = \square$ $8 \times 2 = \square$ $2 \times 11 = \square$

$\square \times 2 = 10$ $2 \times \square = 24$ $\square \times 3 = 6$ $2 \times \square = 24$

STEP 3 (1.5 min) Challenge

Start the timer

Fill in the missing numbers.

$2 \times 3 + 4 = \square$ $8 \times 2 + 3 = \square$ $9 \times 2 + 11 = \square$

$0 \times 2 + 100 = \square$ $7 \times 2 + 16 = \square$ $10 \times 6 - 7 = \square$

$5 \times 8 - \square = 16$ $47 - \square \times 2 = 35$ $65 + 5 \times \square = 100$

Time spent: ________ min ________ sec. Total: ________ out of 40

Practice (1)

Date: ______________________

Day of Week: ______________________

STEP 1 (1 min) Warm-up

Start the timer

Answer these.

59 – 38 = ☐ 86 – 52 = ☐ 28 + 24 = ☐ 25 + 16 = ☐

90 – 29 = ☐ 85 – 27 = ☐ 32 + 18 = ☐ 36 + 45 = ☐

24 + 24 – 17 = ☐ 63 – 5 × 4 = ☐

STEP 2 (2.5 min) Rapid calculation

Start the timer

Answer these.

10 × 2 = ☐ 5 × 4 = ☐ 5 × 10 = ☐ 2 × 3 = ☐

8 × 5 = ☐ 10 × 6 = ☐ 7 × 2 = ☐ 5 × 6 = ☐

2 × 10 = ☐ 2 × 8 = ☐ 4 × 5 = ☐ 10 × 10 = ☐

8 × 2 = ☐ 5 × 5 = ☐ 9 × 10 = ☐ 2 × 7 = ☐

9 × 5 = ☐ 2 × 9 = ☐ 6 × 2 = ☐ 3 × 10 = ☐

STEP 3 (1.5 min) Challenge

Start the timer

Fill in the missing numbers.

16 = 2 × ☐ = 8 × ☐ 15 = ☐ × 5 = ☐ × 3 40 = ☐ × 10 = ☐ × 4

12 = ☐ × 6 = ☐ × 2 35 = ☐ × 7 = ☐ × 5 90 = ☐ × 9 = ☐ × 10

14 = ☐ × 7 = ☐ × 2 45 = 9 × ☐ = 5 × ☐ 70 = ☐ × 7 = 7 × ☐

Time spent: ________ min ________ sec. Total: ________ out of 39

STEP 1 (1 min) Warm-up

Start the timer

Answer these.

60 – 30 = ☐ 80 – 40 = ☐ 25 + 25 = ☐ 45 + 45 = ☐

70 – 31 = ☐ 37 + 26 = ☐ 52 – 28 = ☐ 53 + 29 = ☐

STEP 2 (2.5 min) Rapid calculation

Start the timer

Answer these.

6 × 2 = ☐ 5 × 7 = ☐ 4 × 10 = ☐ 2 × 5 = ☐

3 × 5 = ☐ 10 × 8 = ☐ 4 × 2 = ☐ 5 × 8 = ☐

5 × 10 = ☐ 2 × 6 = ☐ 0 × 5 = ☐ 10 × 0 = ☐

7 × 2 = ☐ 5 × 4 = ☐ 2 × 10 = ☐ 2 × 0 = ☐

11 × 5 = ☐ 2 × 8 = ☐ 5 × 12 = ☐ 11 × 10 = ☐

STEP 3 (1.5 min) Challenge

Start the timer

Fill in the missing numbers.

20 = 2 × ☐ = 10 × ☐

80 = 10 × ☐ = 8 × ☐

20 = 4 × ☐ = 5 × ☐

8 = 8 × ☐ = 1 × ☐

100 = ☐ × 10 = 10 × ☐

40 = ☐ × 8 = ☐ × 5

18 = ☐ × 9 = ☐ × 2

50 = 10 × ☐ = 5 × ☐

30 = 5 × ☐ = 6 × ☐

Time spent: ______ min ______ sec. Total: ______ out of 37

60 Dividing and division (1)

Date: ____________

Day of Week: ____________

STEP 1 (1 min) Warm-up

Start the timer

Answer these.

8 × 5 = ☐ 5 × 2 = ☐ 10 × 4 = ☐ 2 × 9 = ☐ 3 × 5 = ☐

2 × 7 = ☐ 6 × 5 − 16 = ☐ 40 − 2 × 3 = ☐ 8 × 5 + 14 = ☐

STEP 2 (2.5 min) Rapid calculation

Start the timer

Fill in the missing numbers.

1.	4 − 2 − 2 = ☐	4 = ☐ × 2
2.	20 − 5 − 5 − 5 − 5 = ☐	20 = ☐ × 4
3.	15 − 5 − 5 − 5 = ☐	15 = ☐ × 3
4.	40 − 10 − 10 − 10 − 10 = ☐	40 = ☐ × 4
5.	8 − 2 − 2 − 2 − 2 = ☐	8 = ☐ × 4
6.	25 − 5 − 5 − 5 − 5 − 5 = ☐	25 = ☐ × 5
7.	30 − 10 − 10 − 10 = ☐	30 = ☐ × 3
8.	10 − 2 − 2 − 2 − 2 − 2 = ☐	10 = ☐ × 5
9.	50 − 10 − 10 − 10 − 10 − 10 = ☐	50 = ☐ × 5

STEP 3 (1.5 min) Challenge

Start the timer

Fill in the missing numbers.

6 = 2 × ☐	10 = 5 × ☐	20 = 10 × ☐	14 = ☐ × 7
35 = 5 × ☐	60 = ☐ × 6	2 = ☐ × 1	5 = 5 × ☐
10 = 10 × ☐	6 = ☐ × 3	15 = 5 × ☐	40 = 10 × ☐

Time spent: ________ min ________ sec. Total: ________ out of 39

Date: ______________________

Day of Week: ______________________

Dividing and division (2)

STEP 1 (1 min) Warm-up

Start the timer

Answer these.

$10 \times 8 =$ ☐ $8 \times 5 =$ ☐ $2 \times 6 =$ ☐

$3 \times 10 =$ ☐ $2 \times 8 =$ ☐ $27 + 33 =$ ☐

$56 - 26 =$ ☐ $98 - 4 \times 10 =$ ☐ $9 \times 5 + 55 =$ ☐

STEP 2 (2.5 min) Rapid calculation

Start the timer

Fill in the missing numbers.

1. $18 - 2 - 2 - 2 - 2 - 2 - 2 - 2 - 2 - 2 =$ ☐ $18 = 2 \times$ ☐
2. $40 - 5 - 5 - 5 - 5 - 5 - 5 - 5 - 5 =$ ☐ $40 = 5 \times$ ☐
3. $70 - 10 - 10 - 10 - 10 - 10 - 10 - 10 =$ ☐ $70 = 10 \times$ ☐
4. $45 - 5 - 5 - 5 - 5 - 5 - 5 - 5 - 5 - 5 =$ ☐ $45 = 5 \times$ ☐
5. $90 - 10 - 10 - 10 - 10 - 10 - 10 - 10 - 10 - 10 =$ ☐ $90 = 10 \times$ ☐
6. $20 - 2 - 2 - 2 - 2 - 2 - 2 - 2 - 2 - 2 - 2 =$ ☐ $20 = 2 \times$ ☐

STEP 3 (1.5 min) Challenge

Start the timer

Fill in the missing numbers.

$10 = 1 \times$ ☐ $= 2 \times$ ☐ $= 5 \times$ ☐ $20 = 2 \times$ ☐ $= 4 \times$ ☐ $= 10 \times$ ☐

$40 = 4 \times$ ☐ $= 8 \times$ ☐ $50 = 5 \times$ ☐ $= 10 \times$ ☐

Time spent: ________ min ________ sec. Total: ________ out of 25

62 Finding quotients using multiplication facts (1)

Date: ____________

Day of Week: ____________

STEP 1 (1 min) Warm-up

Start the timer

Answer these.

$2 \times 8 =$ ☐ $8 \times 5 =$ ☐ $10 \times 9 =$ ☐ $6 \times 5 =$ ☐

$2 \times 2 + 7 =$ ☐ $5 \times 4 - 6 =$ ☐ $4 \times 10 + 15 =$ ☐ $30 - 7 \times 2 =$ ☐

STEP 2 (2.5 min) Rapid calculation

Start the timer

Answer these.

1. $3 \times 2 =$ ☐ $6 \div 3 =$ ☐ $6 \div 2 =$ ☐
2. $2 \times 4 =$ ☐ $8 \div 2 =$ ☐ $8 \div 4 =$ ☐
3. $5 \times 4 =$ ☐ $20 \div 5 =$ ☐ $20 \div 4 =$ ☐
4. $2 \times 9 =$ ☐ $18 \div 2 =$ ☐ $18 \div 9 =$ ☐
5. $8 \times 5 =$ ☐ $40 \div 8 =$ ☐ $40 \div 5 =$ ☐
6. $7 \times 10 =$ ☐ $70 \div 7 =$ ☐ $70 \div 10 =$ ☐
7. $3 \times 5 =$ ☐ $15 \div 3 =$ ☐ $15 \div 5 =$ ☐
8. $6 \times 10 =$ ☐ $60 \div 10 =$ ☐ $60 \div 6 =$ ☐
9. $7 \times 5 =$ ☐ $35 \div 5 =$ ☐ $35 \div 7 =$ ☐
10. $10 \times 8 =$ ☐ $80 \div 10 =$ ☐ $80 \div 8 =$ ☐
11. $9 \times 5 =$ ☐ $45 \div 5 =$ ☐ $45 \div 9 =$ ☐
12. $2 \times 10 =$ ☐ $20 \div 2 =$ ☐ $20 \div 10 =$ ☐

STEP 3 (1.5 min) Challenge

Start the timer

Answer these.

$10 \div 5 =$ ☐ $12 \div 2 =$ ☐ $40 \div 10 =$ ☐ $16 \div 2 =$ ☐

$70 \div 10 =$ ☐ $14 \div 2 =$ ☐ $40 \div 5 =$ ☐ $100 \div 10 =$ ☐

Time spent: ______ min ______ sec. Total: ______ out of 52

Date: ______________________

Day of Week: ______________________

Finding quotients using multiplication facts (2)

STEP 1 (1 min) Warm-up

Start the timer

Answer these.

$5 \times 6 =$ ☐ $5 \times 10 =$ ☐ $2 \times 9 =$ ☐ $7 \times 10 =$ ☐

$5 \times 9 + 14 =$ ☐ $8 \times 10 - 32 =$ ☐ $24 + 9 \times 2 =$ ☐ $23 - 5 \times 4 =$ ☐

STEP 2 (2.5 min) Rapid calculation

Start the timer

Answer these.

$2 \div 1 =$ ☐ $5 \div 5 =$ ☐ $30 \div 10 =$ ☐ $18 \div 2 =$ ☐

$20 \div 5 =$ ☐ $4 \div 2 =$ ☐ $60 \div 10 =$ ☐ $14 \div 2 =$ ☐

$35 \div 5 =$ ☐ $80 \div 10 =$ ☐ $20 \div 2 =$ ☐ $50 \div 5 =$ ☐

$70 \div 10 =$ ☐ $16 \div 2 =$ ☐ $25 \div 5 =$ ☐ $60 \div 5 =$ ☐

$24 \div 2 =$ ☐ $90 \div 10 =$ ☐ $55 \div 5 =$ ☐ $110 \div 10 =$ ☐

STEP 3 (1.5 min) Challenge

Start the timer

Answer these.

$15 \div 5 + 15 =$ ☐ $2 \times 6 + 12 =$ ☐ $30 \div 10 + 54 =$ ☐

$63 + 16 \div 2 =$ ☐ $16 - 5 \div 5 =$ ☐ $4 \times 10 - 6 =$ ☐

$63 + 35 \div 5 =$ ☐ $11 + 20 \div 2 =$ ☐ $10 \div 10 + 79 =$ ☐

Time spent: ________ min ________ sec. Total: ________ out of 37

64 Division with dividend 0

Date: ______________________

Day of Week: ______________________

STEP 1 (1 min) Warm-up

Start the timer

Answer these.

$4 \times 5 =$ ☐ $3 \times 10 =$ ☐ $8 \times 2 =$ ☐

$10 \times 10 =$ ☐ $10 \div 5 =$ ☐ $2 \times 2 =$ ☐

$10 \times 0 =$ ☐ $40 \div 5 =$ ☐

STEP 2 (2.5 min) Rapid calculation

Start the timer

Answer these.

$0 \div 5 =$ ☐ $0 \times 2 =$ ☐ $0 \div 10 =$ ☐ $2 \times 4 =$ ☐

$5 \div 5 =$ ☐ $0 \div 2 =$ ☐ $2 \div 2 =$ ☐ $10 \div 10 =$ ☐

$0 \times 10 =$ ☐ $5 \times 0 =$ ☐ $23 + 35 \div 5 =$ ☐ $0 \times 10 + 0 =$ ☐

$94 - 6 \times 10 =$ ☐ $0 \times 2 + 77 =$ ☐ $1 \div 1 =$ ☐ $0 \div 5 + 15 =$ ☐

STEP 3 (1.5 min) Challenge

Start the timer

Fill in each box with **>**, **<** or **=**.

$36 + 0$ ☐ $36 - 0$ $10 - 0$ ☐ $0 \div 10$ 0×5 ☐ $0 \div 5$

10×0 ☐ $10 + 0$ $10 + 10$ ☐ 10×10 $5 - 5$ ☐ $5 \div 5$

$0 + 2$ ☐ $0 \div 2$ $2 - 2$ ☐ $0 \div 2$ 0×10 ☐ $10 \div 10$

Time spent: ________ min ________ sec. Total: ________ out of 33

Date: ____________________

Day of Week: ____________________

STEP 1 (1 min) Warm-up

Start the timer

Answer these.

$4 \times 5 =$ ☐	$25 + 4 =$ ☐	$10 \times 5 =$ ☐	$0 \times 2 =$ ☐
$39 + 21 =$ ☐	$46 - 32 =$ ☐	$26 + 14 =$ ☐	$6 \times 10 =$ ☐

STEP 2 (2.5 min) Rapid calculation

Start the timer

Answer these.

$5 \times 7 =$ ☐	$0 \div 2 =$ ☐	$35 \div 5 =$ ☐	$4 \times 10 =$ ☐
$50 \div 5 =$ ☐	$0 \div 10 =$ ☐	$0 \times 10 =$ ☐	$5 \times 7 =$ ☐
$70 \div 10 =$ ☐	$2 \times 7 =$ ☐	$1 \times 5 =$ ☐	$10 \times 0 =$ ☐
$100 \div 10 =$ ☐	$20 \div 2 =$ ☐	$30 \div 5 =$ ☐	$2 \times 10 =$ ☐
$40 \div 5 =$ ☐	$8 \times 2 =$ ☐	$90 \div 10 =$ ☐	$0 \div 5 =$ ☐

STEP 3 (1.5 min) Challenge

Start the timer

Fill in the missing numbers.

$50 \div$ ☐ $= 10$	☐ $\div 7 = 5$	$15 \div$ ☐ $= 3$
☐ $\div 10 = 9$	☐ $- 8 = 6$	☐ $\times 5 = 40$
☐ $\times 2 = 0$	☐ $\div 2 = 10$	☐ $+ 10 = 26$

Time spent: ________ min ________ sec. Total: ________ out of 37

Practice (4)

Date: ____________

Day of Week: ____________

STEP 1 (1 min) Warm-up

Start the timer

Answer these.

40 – 17 = ☐ 35 – 27 = ☐ 38 + 53 = ☐ 27 + 37 = ☐

63 – 28 = ☐ 2 × 2 = ☐ 6 × 10 = ☐ 72 + 8 = ☐

STEP 2 (2.5 min) Rapid calculation

Start the timer

Answer these.

8 ÷ 2 = ☐ 10 ÷ 5 = ☐ 40 ÷ 5 = ☐ 8 × 10 = ☐

20 ÷ 2 = ☐ 0 ÷ 10 = ☐ 0 ÷ 5 = ☐ 9 × 10 = ☐

70 ÷ 10 = ☐ 0 × 5 = ☐ 5 × 10 = ☐ 0 × 2 = ☐

45 ÷ 5 = ☐ 18 ÷ 2 = ☐ 0 ÷ 2 = ☐ 10 ÷ 10 = ☐

2 × 10 = ☐ 5 × 10 = ☐ 8 × 2 = ☐ 10 × 9 = ☐

STEP 3 (1.5 min) Challenge

Start the timer

Fill in the missing numbers.

☐ × 5 = 35 ☐ × 0 = 0 ☐ ÷ 2 = 0

5 × ☐ = 30 8 × ☐ = 40 ☐ ÷ 10 = 7

☐ × 7 = 35 ÷ 5 80 ÷ 10 = ☐ × 2 8 × 5 = ☐ × 4

Time spent: ________ min ________ sec. Total: ________ out of 37

Date: ______________________

Day of Week: ______________________

STEP 1 (1 min) Warm-up

Start the timer

Answer these.

44 + 29 = ☐	24 + 73 = ☐	38 – 19 = ☐	68 – 15 = ☐
10 × 8 = ☐	3 × 5 = ☐	2 × 5 = ☐	7 × 10 = ☐
2 × 10 = ☐	10 × 5 = ☐	0 × 5 = ☐	8 × 2 = ☐

STEP 2 (2.5 min) Rapid calculation

Start the timer

Answer these.

80 ÷ 8 = ☐	15 ÷ 5 = ☐	12 ÷ 6 = ☐	5 × 4 = ☐
20 ÷ 4 = ☐	0 × 10 = ☐	50 ÷ 5 = ☐	4 × 2 = ☐
0 ÷ 10 = ☐	8 × 5 = ☐	5 × 0 = ☐	1 × 1 = ☐
5 ÷ 1 = ☐	100 ÷ 10 = ☐	40 ÷ 5 = ☐	18 ÷ 2 = ☐
10 × 2 + 36 = ☐	100 – 10 × 10 = ☐	30 ÷ 10 + 29 = ☐	25 + 7 × 10 = ☐

STEP 3 (1.5 min) Challenge

Start the timer

Fill in each box with **>**, **<** or **=**.

12 – 0 ☐ 0 ÷ 10	2 + 0 ☐ 0 × 2	0 ÷ 5 ☐ 5 – 0
40 + 0 ☐ 40 – 0	10 × 0 ☐ 0 ÷ 10	5 – 5 ☐ 5 ÷ 5
20 ÷ 2 ☐ 45 ÷ 5	3 × 5 ☐ 2 × 8	60 ÷ 10 ☐ 25 ÷ 5

Time spent: ________ min ________ sec. Total: ________ out of 41

68 Commutative law of multiplication

Date: ______

Day of Week: ______

STEP 1 (1 min) Warm-up

Start the timer

Answer these.

1. 2 × 6 = ☐
   6 × 2 = ☐
2. 4 × 5 = ☐
   5 × 4 = ☐
3. 7 × 10 = ☐
   10 × 7 = ☐
4. 8 × 2 = ☐
   2 × 8 = ☐
5. 9 × 5 = ☐
   5 × 9 = ☐
6. 10 × 9 = ☐
   9 × 10 = ☐

STEP 2 (2.5 min) Rapid calculation

Start the timer

Fill in the missing numbers.

5 × 3 = 3 × ☐ = ☐

10 × 4 = 4 × ☐ = ☐

2 × 7 = 7 × ☐ = ☐

10 × 6 = 6 × ☐ = ☐

5 × 7 = 7 × ☐ = ☐

2 × 9 = 9 × ☐ = ☐

10 × 8 = ☐ × ☐ = ☐

4 × 2 = ☐ × ☐ = ☐

5 × 8 = ☐ × ☐ = ☐

10 × 2 = ☐ × ☐ = ☐

5 × 6 = ☐ × ☐ = ☐

10 × 5 = ☐ × ☐ = ☐

STEP 3 (1.5 min) Challenge

Start the timer

Fill in the missing numbers.

9 × ☐ = ☐ = ☐ × 5

8 × ☐ = ☐ = ☐ × 2

3 × ☐ = ☐ = ☐ × 10

6 × ☐ = ☐ = ☐ × 2

9 × ☐ = ☐ = ☐ × 10

7 × ☐ = ☐ = ☐ × 5

7 × ☐ = ☐ = ☐ × 10

8 × ☐ = ☐ = ☐ × 5

Time spent: ______ min ______ sec. Total: ______ out of 32

Date: ____________________

Day of Week: ____________________

Subtraction and division are not commutative

STEP 1 (1 min) Warm-up

Start the timer

Do these calculations have the same answer? Write **yes** or **no** next to each one.

12 + 5 and 5 + 12 ____________

5 × 7 and 7 × 5 ____________

10 – 3 and 3 – 10 ____________

10 ÷ 2 and 2 ÷ 10 ____________

18 – 6 and 6 – 18 ____________

8 × 2 and 2 × 8 ____________

40 ÷ 5 and 5 ÷ 40 ____________

33 + 50 and 50 + 33 ____________

STEP 2 (2.5 min) Rapid calculation

Start the timer

1. Fill in the missing numbers.

13 + 6 = 6 + ☐ = ☐

7 × 5 = 5 × ☐ = ☐

26 + 30 = 30 + ☐ = ☐

9 × 10 = 10 × ☐ = ☐

34 + 8 = 8 + ☐ = ☐

2 × 7 = 7 × ☐ = ☐

2. Fill in the missing numbers. The first one has been done for you.

12 – 9 does not equal 9 – **12**

50 ÷ ☐ does not equal 5 ÷ 50

☐ – 60 does not equal 60 – 96

15 ÷ 5 does not equal 5 ÷ ☐

20 ÷ ☐ does not equal 2 ÷ 20

☐ ÷ 10 does not equal 10 ÷ 60

STEP 3 (1.5 min) Challenge

Start the timer

Fill in the missing numbers so that the four calculations in each set give the same answer.

1. ☐ + 6 = 23 – ☐ = 2 × ☐ = 20 ÷ ☐ = 10

2. ☐ + 0 = 83 – ☐ = 4 × ☐ = 80 ÷ ☐ = 8

3. 4 + ☐ = ☐ – 58 = 1 × ☐ = ☐ ÷ 5 = 4

4. ☐ + 1 = ☐ – 77 = 3 × ☐ = ☐ ÷ 2 = 6

Time spent: ________ min ________ sec. Total: ________ out of 23

70 General review (9)

Date: ______________________

Day of Week: ______________________

STEP 1 (1 min) Warm-up

Start the timer

Answer these.

1. 14 + 9 = ☐	**2.** 27 + 6 = ☐	**3.** 39 + 5 = ☐	**4.** 27 + 36 = ☐
23 − 9 = ☐	33 − 6 = ☐	44 − 5 = ☐	63 − 36 = ☐
23 − 14 = ☐	33 − 27 = ☐	44 − 39 = ☐	63 − 27 = ☐

STEP 2 (2.5 min) Rapid calculation

Start the timer

Answer these.

51 − 37 = ☐	33 − 26 = ☐	45 + 28 = ☐	65 + 27 = ☐
34 + 48 = ☐	96 − 48 = ☐	27 + 39 = ☐	84 − 36 = ☐
72 − 58 = ☐	18 + 49 = ☐	69 + 23 = ☐	79 + 14 = ☐
63 − 49 = ☐	93 − 47 = ☐	36 + 49 = ☐	58 + 25 = ☐
52 − 24 = ☐	18 + 38 = ☐	83 − 54 = ☐	55 − 26 = ☐

STEP 3 (1.5 min) Challenge

Start the timer

Fill in the missing numbers.

☐ + 67 = 81	21 + ☐ = 40	92 = 94 − ☐
☐ − 24 = 75	85 − ☐ = 38	☐ + 38 = 65
100 − ☐ = 31	☐ − 35 = 48	78 + ☐ + 12 = 100

Time spent: ________ min ________ sec. Total: ________ out of 41

Date: ____________________

Day of Week: ____________________

General review (10) 71

STEP 1 (1 min) Warm-up

Start the timer

Answer these.

37 + 24 = 40 + ☐

63 + 37 = ☐ + 40

44 + 38 = ☐ + 40

29 + 42 = 30 + ☐

47 + 46 = 50 + ☐

66 − 27 = ☐ − 30

41 − 22 = ☐ − 20

74 − 58 = ☐ − 60

45 − 29 = ☐ − 30

91 − 23 = ☐ − 20

STEP 2 (2.5 min) Rapid calculation

Start the timer

Fill in the missing numbers. Some have been done for you.

46 + 46 = **50** + **42** = ☐

37 + 48 = ☐ + ☐ = ☐

24 + 67 = ☐ + ☐ = ☐

52 + 19 = ☐ + ☐ = ☐

29 + 63 = ☐ + ☐ = ☐

76 + 14 = ☐ + ☐ = ☐

74 − 46 = **78** − **50** = ☐

53 − 24 = ☐ − ☐ = ☐

75 − 57 = ☐ − ☐ = ☐

72 − 23 = ☐ − ☐ = ☐

64 − 36 = ☐ − ☐ = ☐

82 − 48 = ☐ − ☐ = ☐

STEP 3 (1.5 min) Challenge

Start the timer

Answer these.

86 − 48 = ☐

44 − 17 = ☐

76 − 37 = ☐

73 − 59 + 28 = ☐

68 + 14 = ☐

35 + 36 = ☐

44 + 29 = ☐

97 − 43 − 25 = ☐

64 + 28 − 53 = ☐

15 + 24 + 36 = ☐

Time spent: ______ min ______ sec. Total: ______ out of 32

72 General review (11)

Date: ______

Day of Week: ______

STEP 1 (1 min) Warm-up

Start the timer

Fill in the missing numbers.

32 + 24 = ☐ + 20

41 + 28 = 40 + ☐

53 + 37 = 50 + ☐

62 + 29 = 60 + ☐

65 – 46 = ☐ – 50

75 – 58 = ☐ – 60

62 – 28 = ☐ – 30

32 – 24 = ☐ – 30

45 + 23 = ☐ + 20

64 – 27 = ☐ – 30

STEP 2 (2.5 min) Rapid calculation

Start the timer

Fill in the missing numbers. The first one has been done for you.

55 – 18 = **57** – **20** = **37**

43 + 19 = ☐ + ☐ = ☐

23 + 18 = ☐ + ☐ = ☐

52 + 19 = ☐ + ☐ = ☐

24 + 68 = ☐ + ☐ = ☐

19 + 43 = ☐ + ☐ = ☐

52 – 14 = ☐ – ☐ = ☐

74 – 15 = ☐ – ☐ = ☐

37 – 29 = ☐ – ☐ = ☐

47 + 27 = ☐ + ☐ = ☐

34 + 18 = ☐ + ☐ = ☐

65 – 27 = ☐ – ☐ = ☐

92 – 35 = ☐ – ☐ = ☐

STEP 3 (1.5 min) Challenge

Start the timer

Answer these.

31 – 18 = ☐

42 + 19 = ☐

56 – 38 = ☐

67 – 19 + 28 = ☐

43 – 24 = ☐

72 + 23 = ☐

28 + 56 = ☐

24 + 27 + 16 = ☐

46 – 15 – 22 = ☐

18 + 36 – 29 = ☐

Time spent: ______ min ______ sec. Total: ______ out of 32

Date: ____________________

Day of Week: ____________________

General review (12)

STEP 1 (1 min) Warm-up

Start the timer

Answer these.

24 + 30 = ☐ 55 – 25 = ☐ 46 + 30 = ☐ 59 – 40 = ☐

80 – 45 = ☐ 90 – 60 = ☐ 26 + 40 = ☐ 65 – 25 = ☐

73 – 33 = ☐ 45 + 50 = ☐ 100 – 15 = ☐

STEP 2 (2.5 min) Rapid calculation

Start the timer

Fill in the missing numbers.

☐ + 4 = 20 7 + ☐ = 57 ☐ + 7 = 15 ☐ + 9 = 12

9 + ☐ = 39 16 + ☐ = 47 ☐ + 26 = 56 ☐ + 27 = 58

☐ + 37 = 79 ☐ + 45 = 98 14 + ☐ = 68 56 + ☐ = 77

56 + ☐ = 98 ☐ + 25 = 50 ☐ + 15 = 76 23 + ☐ = 59

STEP 3 (1.5 min) Challenge

Start the timer

Fill in the missing numbers.

☐ + 48 = 67 ☐ + 15 = 51 ☐ + 53 = 60

49 + ☐ = 61 62 + ☐ = 100 58 + ☐ = 58

☐ + 36 = 71 47 + ☐ = 76 ☐ + 45 = 65

12 + ☐ = 81 ☐ + 44 = 79

Time spent: ______ min ______ sec. Total: ______ out of 38

74 General review (13)

Date: ______

Day of Week: ______

STEP 1 (1 min) Warm-up

Start the timer

Answer these.

1. 41 + 29 = ☐

29 + 41 = ☐

70 − 29 = ☐

70 − 41 = ☐

2. 53 + 28 = ☐

28 + 53 = ☐

81 − 28 = ☐

81 − 53 = ☐

3. 92 − 54 = ☐

54 + 38 = ☐

4. 74 + 24 = ☐

98 − 74 = ☐

STEP 2 (2.5 min) Rapid calculation

Start the timer

Fill in the mssing numbers.

☐ − 8 = 20	☐ − 5 = 57	☐ − 7 = 14	☐ − 9 = 12
☐ − 6 = 39	64 − ☐ = 43	41 − ☐ = 20	37 − ☐ = 28
71 − ☐ = 41	45 − ☐ = 12	64 − ☐ = 27	83 − ☐ = 7
☐ + 18 = 98	☐ − 25 = 50	☐ − 15 = 15	☐ − 17 = 12

STEP 3 (1.5 min) Challenge

Start the timer

Fill in the missing numbers.

☐ − 28 = 47	☐ − 57 = 36	☐ − 27 = 64
68 − ☐ = 44	43 − ☐ = 25	35 − ☐ = 35
☐ − 37 = 63	100 − ☐ = 76	☐ − 34 = 34
85 − ☐ = 62	☐ − 11 = 85	

Time spent: ______ min ______ sec. Total: ______ out of 39

Date: ____________________

Day of Week: ____________________

General review (14) 75

STEP 1 (1 min) Warm-up

Start the timer

Answer these.

32 + 16 = ☐	32 – 16 = ☐	7 × 5 = ☐	8 × 8 = ☐
15 ÷ 5 = ☐	20 ÷ 2 = ☐	100 – 26 = ☐	81 – 39 = ☐
24 + 37 = ☐	80 ÷ 10 = ☐	30 ÷ 5 = ☐	10 × 7 = ☐

STEP 2 (2.5 min) Rapid calculation

Start the timer

Answer these.

10 × 4 = ☐	8 × 5 = ☐	35 ÷ 5 = ☐	14 ÷ 2 = ☐
4 × 5 = ☐	8 × 2 = ☐	25 ÷ 5 = ☐	90 ÷ 10 = ☐
8 × 10 = ☐	2 × 5 = ☐	45 ÷ 5 = ☐	30 ÷ 10 = ☐
8 × 5 = ☐	6 × 10 = ☐	18 ÷ 2 = ☐	40 ÷ 5 = ☐
5 × 9 = ☐	10 × 10 = ☐	12 ÷ 2 = ☐	70 ÷ 10 = ☐

STEP 3 (1.5 min) Challenge

Start the timer

Answer these.

2 × 10 + 31 = ☐	30 ÷ 5 – 2 = ☐	2 × 8 + 15 = ☐
5 × 10 + 28 = ☐	10 ÷ 2 + 9 = ☐	9 × 5 – 19 = ☐
10 × 4 + 59 = ☐	40 ÷ 5 – 7 = ☐	0 ÷ 6 + 78 = ☐

Time spent: ________ min ________ sec. Total: ________ out of 41

76 General review (15)

Date: ____________________

Day of Week: ____________________

STEP 1 (1 min) Warm-up

Start the timer

Answer these.

27 + 16 = ☐	39 – 15 = ☐	4 × 2 = ☐	7 × 2 = ☐
50 ÷ 5 = ☐	40 ÷ 10 = ☐	34 – 17 = ☐	31 – 12 = ☐
26 + 49 = ☐	12 ÷ 2 = ☐	50 ÷ 10 = ☐	5 × 5 = ☐

STEP 2 (2.5 min) Rapid calculation

Start the timer

Answer these.

10 × 3 = ☐	40 ÷ 5 = ☐	50 ÷ 10 = ☐	20 ÷ 5 = ☐
10 × 6 = ☐	10 ÷ 5 = ☐	6 ÷ 2 = ☐	60 ÷ 10 = ☐
1 × 5 = ☐	100 ÷ 10 = ☐	2 ÷ 2 = ☐	5 ÷ 5 = ☐
82 – 19 = ☐	36 + 47 = ☐	35 + 65 = ☐	0 ÷ 10 = ☐
3 + 59 = ☐	100 – 63 = ☐	41 – 36 = ☐	53 – 28 = ☐

STEP 3 (1.5 min) Challenge

Start the timer

Answer these.

7 × 5 + 35 = ☐	10 × 10 – 45 = ☐	10 × 2 – 18 = ☐
8 × 5 – 22 = ☐	4 × 10 + 48 = ☐	5 × 9 + 45 = ☐
5 × 0 + 91 = ☐	0 ÷ 10 + 18 = ☐	2 × 5 × 10 = ☐

Time spent: ________ min ________ sec. Total: ________ out of 41

Date: ______

Day of Week: ______

General review (16)

STEP 1 (1 min) Warm-up

Start the timer

Answer these.

$4 + 36 = \square$	$54 - 5 = \square$	$10 \times 0 = \square$	$0 \times 2 = \square$
$10 \div 10 = \square$	$30 \div 5 = \square$	$50 - 18 = \square$	$33 + 12 = \square$
$26 + 24 = \square$	$20 \div 10 = \square$	$4 \div 2 = \square$	$1 \times 10 = \square$

STEP 2 (2.5 min) Rapid calculation

Start the timer

Answer these.

$10 \times 2 = \square$	$5 \div 1 = \square$	$10 \div 1 = \square$	$2 \div 1 = \square$
$62 - 19 = \square$	$8 \div 2 = \square$	$13 + 64 = \square$	$16 \div 2 = \square$
$100 - 19 = \square$	$40 \div 5 + 3 = \square$	$30 \div 10 + 5 = \square$	$8 + 78 = \square$
$40 \div 5 + 57 = \square$	$60 \div 10 - 2 = \square$	$20 \div 2 + 87 = \square$	$25 \div 5 + 55 = \square$
$70 \div 10 + 33 = \square$	$18 - 18 \div 2 = \square$	$0 \times 10 + 77 = \square$	$0 \div 2 + 91 = \square$

STEP 3 (1.5 min) Challenge

Start the timer

Find the largest number that can be filled in each box.

$5 \times \square < 55$	$2 \times \square < 5$	$8 \times \square < 42$	$4 \times \square < 43$
$10 \times \square < 49$	$4 \times \square < 9$	$5 \times \square < 53$	$10 \times \square < 109$

Time spent: ______ min ______ sec. Total: ______ out of 40

78 General review (17)

Date: ____________________

Day of Week: ____________________

STEP 1 (1 min) Warm-up

Start the timer

Answer these.

2 × 10 + 5 = □ 4 × 5 + 15 = □ 9 × 2 − 6 = □ 5 × 8 − 10 = □

53 − 18 = □ 61 − 57 = □ 45 + 36 = □ 38 + 27 = □

0 ÷ 4 + 12 = □ 35 − 10 × 0 = □

STEP 2 (2.5 min) Rapid calculation

Start the timer

1. Answer these.

35 ÷ 5 − 5 = □ 80 ÷ 10 + 17 = □ 18 ÷ 2 − 5 = □ 45 ÷ 5 + 8 = □

90 − 10 ÷ 10 = □ 41 + 5 × 5 = □ 27 + 0 ÷ 2 = □ 70 − 0 × 5 = □

2. Find the largest number that can be filled in each box.

7 × □ < 71 8 × □ < 23 2 × □ < 17 9 × □ < 53

3 × □ < 32 5 × □ < 29 6 × □ < 35 4 × □ < 43

STEP 3 (1.5 min) Challenge

Start the timer

Fill in the missing numbers.

□ × 10 = 0 5 × □ = 40 2 ÷ □ = 1

39 = □ × 7 + 4 7 = □ × □ − 3 □ × 8 = 20 − 4

□ ÷ 5 = 37 − 28 □ × 6 = 100 − 40 3 + 17 + 5 = □ × □

Time spent: ________ min ________ sec. Total: ________ out of 35

Date: ____________________

Day of Week: ____________________

General review (18) 79

STEP 1 (1 min) Warm-up

Start the timer

Potted plants are arranged in equal rows. How many plants are there in total?

	Total number of plants
4 rows of 5 plants	
3 rows of 10 plants	
5 rows of 8 plants	

	Total number of plants
6 rows of 2 plants	
2 rows of 9 plants	
10 rows of 9 plants	

STEP 2 (2.5 min) Rapid calculation

Start the timer

Which has more beads? Circle the correct answer in each pair.

2 bags of 8 beads **or** 3 bags of 5 beads

9 bags of 2 beads **or** 2 bags of 10 beads

6 bags of 2 beads **or** 1 bag of 10 beads

5 bags of 10 beads **or** 10 bags of 4 beads

5 bags of 8 beads **or** 3 bags of 10 beads

4 bags of 10 beads **or** 7 bags of 5 beads

5 bags of 9 beads **or** 8 bags of 5 beads

5 bags of 7 beads **or** 8 bags of 5 beads

7 bags of 2 beads **or** 2 bags of 8 beads

5 bags of 5 beads **or** 10 bags of 3 beads

STEP 3 (1.5 min) Challenge

Start the timer

1. There are 10 groups of 5 children. How many more children will make 63? ☐

2. There are 8 groups of 2 children. How many more children will make 31? ☐

3. There are 7 groups of 10 children. How many more children will make 94? ☐

4. There are 5 groups of 9 children. How many more children will make 68? ☐

Time spent: ________ min ________ sec. Total: ________ out of 20

80 General review (19)

Date: ______________________

Day of Week: ______________________

STEP 1 (1 min) Warm-up

Start the timer

How many counters are in each tray?

20 counters shared equally between 2 trays ☐

18 counters shared equally between 9 trays ☐

60 counters shared equally between 10 trays ☐

90 counters shared equally between 10 trays ☐

30 counters shared equally between 5 trays ☐

45 counters shared equally between 5 trays ☐

STEP 2 (2.5 min) Rapid calculation

Start the timer

Seeds are planted in equal rows. How many seeds are in each row?

35 seeds in 5 rows ☐

16 seeds in 2 rows ☐

12 seeds in 6 rows ☐

40 seeds in 4 rows ☐

20 seeds in 4 rows ☐

80 seeds in 10 rows ☐

50 seeds in 5 rows ☐

15 seeds in 3 rows ☐

20 seeds in 2 rows ☐

100 seeds in 10 rows ☐

STEP 3 (1.5 min) Challenge

Start the timer

1. £50 is shared equally between 5 boys. Each boy needs £ ☐ more to have £13.
2. £60 is shared equally between 10 girls. Each girl needs £ ☐ more to have £24.
3. £18 is shared equally between 2 boys. Each boy needs £ ☐ more to have £31.
4. £45 is shared equally between 9 girls. Each girl needs £ ☐ more to have £42.
5. £90 is shared equally between 9 boys. Each boy needs £ ☐ more to have £73.
6. £16 is shared equally between 8 girls. Each girl needs £ ☐ more to have £62.

Time spent: ________ min ________ sec. Total: ________ out of 22

ANSWERS

Test 1

Step 1:
From top left, left to right: 13; 9; 15; 2; 6; 13; 20; 10; 17; 5

Step 2:
From top left, left to right: 20; 9; 17; 18; 12; 21; 20; 8; 18; 12; 11; 0; 15; 19; 7; 14; 8; 15; 5; 10

Step 3:
From top left, left to right: 8; 11; 9; 8; 2; 6; 14; 6

Test 2

Step 1:
From top left, left to right: 13; 7; 17; 5; 13; 5; 8; 13; 10; 2

Step 2:
From top left, left to right: 6; 17; 13; 11; 16; 13; 20; 7; 19; 2; 16; 16; 9; 7; 16; 13; 9; 14; 8; 9

Step 3:
From top left, left to right: 14; 9; 9; 0; 4; 8; 18; 9

Test 3

Step 1:
First column: 11p; 15p; 17p; 6p; 17p
Second column: £11; £2; £19; £11; £17

Step 2:
First column: 4 m; 12 m; 7 m; 15 m; 5 m; 8 cm; 18 cm; 9 cm; 16 cm; 7 cm
Second column: 19 m; 18 m; 7 m; 1 m; 18 m; 20 cm; 16 cm; 7 cm; 2 cm; 18 cm

Step 3:
From top left, left to right: 12 cm; 12 cm; 7 cm; 9 cm; 4 m; 9 m; 11 m; 5 m

Test 4

Step 1:
From top left, left to right: 15; 10; 19; 10; 14; 15; 13; 10; 7; 7

Step 2:
From top left, left to right: <; >; =; <; <; <; =; >; <; =; >; >; =; =; >; <

Step 3:
From top left, left to right: 1; 9; 9; 4; 13; 5; 15; 10

Test 5

Step 1:
From top left, left to right: 70; 90; 80; 90; 72; 95; 84; 97

Step 2:
From top left, left to right: 72; 95; 84; 97; 97; 88; 93; 77; 85; 91; 49; 82; 72; 55; 49; 55; 83; 86; 71; 100

Step 3:
From top left, left to right: 30; 40; 20; 48; 60; 29; 30; 35; 48

Test 6

Step 1:
From top left, left to right: 15; 53; 71; 33; 58; 57; 59; 91

Step 2:
1. 58; 31; 95; 66; 43; 74; 97; 45; 91; 90
2. >; <; <; >; >; =; >; =

Step 3:
From top left, left to right: 40; 35; 20; 30; 74; 30; 50; 30; 37

Test 7

Step 1:
First column: £17; £46; £83; £59; £65
Second column: 36p; 48p; 92p; 97p; 70p

Step 2:
1. First column: 57 m; 75 m; 85 m; 63 m
Second column: 67 cm; 84 cm; 82 cm; 65 cm
2. From top left, left to right: <; =; <; >; =; >; =; <

Step 3:
From top left, left to right: 20 m; 42 m; 40 m; 30 cm; 49 cm; 40 cm; 10 m; 20 cm; 56 m

Test 8

Step 1:
From top left, left to right: 40; 70; 20; 30; 41; 77; 26; 34

Step 2:
From top left, left to right: 41; 77; 26; 34; 57; 28; 33; 27; 45; 11; 29; 22; 2; 45; 45; 5; 7; 11; 31; 0

Step 3:
From top left, left to right: 33; 78; 82; 70; 40; 96; 50; 30; 57

Test 9

Step 1:
From top left, left to right: 5; 47; 69; 27; 42; 48; 19; 39

Step 2:
1. 71; 55; 74; 26; 38; 7; 29; 11; 9; 10
2. <; <; >; <; >; <; >; >

Step 3:
From top left, left to right: 30; 30; 69; 70; 62; 39; 50; 50; 55

Answers

Test 10

Step 1:

First column: £25; £36; £58; £64; £41

Second column: 57p; 43p; 28p; 15p; 14p

Step 2:

1. First column: 12 m; 38 m; 59 m; 11 m
   Second column: 27 cm; 26 cm; 5 cm; 19 cm
2. <; >; =; <; <; >; =; <

Step 3:

From top left, left to right: 26 m; 27 m; 69 m; 53 cm; 62 cm; 93 cm; 43 m; 18 cm; 55 m

Test 11

Step 1:

From top left, left to right: 8; 9; 7; 9; 60; 80; 80; 47

Step 2:

From top left, left to right: 89; 55; 79; 69; 58; 49; 89; 39; 38; 69; 57; 46; 68; 29; 47; 59; 68; 29; 47; 59

Step 3:

From top left, left to right: 60; 90; 60; 71; 51; 43; 40; 81; 6

Test 12

Step 1:

From top left, left to right: 76; 90; 92; 90; 17; 39; 34; 59

Step 2:

1. From top left, left to right: 49; 58; 78; 68; 79; 19; 87; 88; 49; 45
2. From top left, left to right: =; <; =; >; =; <; >; <

Step 3:

From top left, left to right: 4; 5; 33; 6; 51; 91; 3; 5; 4

Test 13

Step 1:

From top left, left to right: 3; 1; 5; 2; 53; 71; 45; 92

Step 2:

From top left, left to right: 14; 23; 39; 45; 51; 77; 58; 69; 59; 59; 59; 59; 52; 54; 56; 58; 53; 71; 45; 92

Step 3:

From top left, left to right: 42; 77; 38; 55; 56; 90; 88; 68; 2

Test 14

Step 1:

From top left, left to right: 45; 25; 41; 68; 85; 19; 29; 39

Step 2:

1. From top left, left to right: 23; 78; 36; 88; 57; 45; 69; 25; 49; 59
2. From top left, left to right: <; <; >; <; <; =; =; >

Step 3:

From top left, left to right: 6; 82; 7; 25; 8; 7; 57; 9; 28

Test 15

Step 1:

From top left, left to right: 61; 37; 51; 84; 92; 28; 49; 66

Step 2:

From top left, left to right: 59; 68; 35; 68; 34; 34; 73; 81; 70; 70; 70; 60; 66; 48; 30; 70; 77; 35

Step 3:

From top left, left to right: 5; 40; 5; 73; 9; 7; 6; 7; 82

Test 16

Step 1:

1. 73, 73
2. 79, 79
3. 64, 64
4. 67, 67
5. 59, 59

Step 2:

From top left, left to right: 80; 63; 70; 76; 98; 51; 56; 86; 37; 81; 56; 62; 34; 73; 62; 64; 41; 42; 71; 35

Step 3:

From top left, left to right: 41; 8; 7; 46; 59; 2; 9; 7; 8

Test 17

Step 1:

First column: £71; £52; £67; £82; £92

Second column: 54p; 46p; 88p; 68p; 37p

Step 2:

First column: 48 m; 51 m; 74 m; 67 m; 15 cm; 43 cm; 62 cm; 74 cm; 86 cm

Second column: 81 m; 58 m; 67 m; 70 m; 39 cm; 65 cm; 62 cm; 98 cm; 99 cm

Step 3:

From top left, left to right: £8; £38; £35; £36; £29; £34; £22; £20; £72

Test 18

Step 1:

From top left, left to right: 7; 8; 80; 80; 90; 90; 40; 86

Step 2:

From top left, left to right: 91; 87; 85; 84; 95; 85; 45; 79; 67; 96; 97; 84; 42; 86; 68; 26; 89; 97; 98; 46

Step 3:

From top left, left to right: 33; 55; 77; 55; 77; 99; 70; 28; 22

Test 19

Step 1:
From top left, left to right: 51; 84; 56; 98; 98; 30; 90; 80
Step 2:
From top left, left to right: 80; 90; 80; 80; 85; 85; 85; 85; 74; 74; 91; 91; 58; 96; 74; 52; 80; 90
Step 3:
From top left, left to right: 41; 61; 81; 52; 72; 92; 43; 93; 94

Test 20

Step 1:
From top left, left to right: 54; 86; 59; 100; 99; 31; 92; 84
Step 2:
From top left, left to right: 76; 54; 98; 32; 83; 83; 83; 83; 32; 52; 72; 92; 93; 67; 81; 91; 82; 91
Step 3:
From top left, left to right: 53; 86; 75; 71; 73; 75; 61; 63; 65

Test 21

Step 1:
From top left, left to right: 66; 99; 88; 99; 33; 84; 81; 93
Step 2:
From top left, left to right: 34; 97; 80; 80; 64; 64; 97; 86; 63; 98; 99; 93; 90; 66; 85; 91; 70; 98
Step 3:
From top left, left to right: 76; 91; 72; 27; 58; 23; 41; 38; 55

Test 22

Step 1:
From top left, left to right: 10; 60; 50; 20; 20; 12; 64; 53
Step 2:
From top left, left to right: 46; 20; 40; 80; 13; 61; 33; 42; 71; 45; 65; 23; 53; 0; 39; 41; 25; 21
Step 3:
From top left, left to right: 66; 44; 22; 73; 53; 33; 50; 88; 41

Test 23

Step 1:
From top left, left to right: 11; 24; 24; 38; 18; 4; 50; 30
Step 2:
From top left, left to right: 31; 23; 40; 52; 38; 29; 39; 49; 29; 29; 29; 29; 66; 46; 26; 6; 4; 24
Step 3:
From top left, left to right: 9; 19; 29; 11; 18; 27; 36; 13; 65

Test 24

Step 1:
From top left, left to right: 7; 22; 20; 36; 17; 5; 28; 0
Step 2:
From top left, left to right: 45; 45; 45; 45; 65; 47; 25; 5; 18; 6; 24; 35; 34; 9; 38; 28; 37; 18
Step 3:
From top left, left to right: 17; 29; 45; 35; 37; 39; 23; 25; 27

Test 25

Step 1:
From top left, left to right: 18; 45; 18; 9; 9; 28; 59; 26
Step 2:
From top left, left to right: 16; 6; 20; 3; 17; 34; 23; 59; 48; 0; 68; 28; 34; 36; 49; 23; 22; 0
Step 3:
From top left, left to right: 40; 35; 15; 53; 22; 27; 39; 92; 87

Test 26

Step 1:
From top left, left to right: 73; 19; 26; 97; 95; 21; 87; 94
Step 2:
From top left, left to right: 99; 30; 88; 50; 90; 90; 21; 27; 81; 55; 90; 65; 0; 67; 18; 78; 72; 80
Step 3:
From top left, left to right: 49; 51; 29; 63; 26; 36; 15; 52; 70

Test 27

Step 1:
From top left, left to right: 37; 43; 53; 48; 25; 84; 38; 91
Step 2:
From top left, left to right: 72; 96; 27; 16; 44; 78; 62; 71; 27; 97; 17; 86; 30; 57; 61; 57; 35; 50
Step 3:
From top left, left to right: 32; 32; 35; 18; 52; 70; 36; 53; 75

Test 28

Step 1:
From top left, left to right: 75; 9; 44; 63; 47; 48; 60; 30
Step 2:
From top left, left to right: 20; 72; 73; 45; 82; 45; 86; 28; 14; 67; 92; 65; 14; 43; 88; 83; 60; 45
Step 3:
From top left, left to right: 14; 19; 12; 99; 47; 27; 63; 99; 5

Answers

Test 29

Step 1:
From top left, left to right: 50; 60; 70; 80; 90; 18; 27; 36
Step 2:
From top left, left to right: 94; 0; 17; 85; 47; 95; 38; 83; 80; 29; 46; 93; 82; 97; 39; 33; 45; 45
Step 3:
From top left, left to right: 70; 37; 62; 92; 19; 34; 30; 64; 0

Test 30

Step 1:
First column: £50; £40; £70; £70; £90
Second column: 19p; 27p; 29p; 39p; 5p
Step 2:
First column: 58 m; 38 m; 48 cm; 15 cm; 90 m; 84 m; 91 cm; 57 cm; 65 cm
Second column: 20 m; 93 m; 75 cm; 75 cm; 19 m; 70 m; 78 cm; 21 cm; 55 cm
Step 3:
From top left, left to right: £60; £45; £33; £72; £18; £38; 61p; 87p; 24p

Test 31

Step 1:
From top left, left to right: 13; 13; 11; 12; 13; 16; 15; 14
Step 2:
From top left, left to right: 11; 12; 12; 11; 19; 18; 14; 15; 17; 18; 19; 17; 15; 18; 15; 16; 13; 12
Step 3:
From top left, left to right: 25; 25; 24; 20; 22; 27; 21; 24

Test 32

Step 1:
From top left, left to right: 12; 12; 12; 15; 16; 18; 20; 21
Step 2:
From top left, left to right: 17; 20; 16; 17; 14; 22; 15; 18; 18; 15; 19; 27; 20; 21; 12; 12; 16; 9
Step 3:
From top left, left to right: 2; 6; 5; 9; 9; 5; 9; 0

Test 33

Step 1:
From top left, left to right: 11; 10; 15; 15; 18; 18; 21; 24
Step 2:
From top left, left to right: 11; 12; 18; 13; 20; 18; 21; 18; 19; 21; 18; 17; 24; 24; 13; 17; 18; 18
Step 3:
From top left, left to right: 3; 7; 7; 0; 2; 6; 4; 4

Test 34

Step 1:
From top left, left to right: 35; 88; 79; 87; 5; 62; 34; 40
Step 2:
From top left, left to right: 72; 96; 27; 19; 44; 78; 62; 71; 26; 14; 17; 28; 4; 81; 23; 66; 91; 5
Step 3:
From top left, left to right: 22; 22; 26; 18; 28; 53; 16; 63; 75

Test 35

Step 1:
From top left, left to right: 54; 74; 98; 91; 42; 74; 63; 95
Step 2:
From top left, left to right: 80 + 12 = 92; 70 + 21 = 91; 41 + 30 = 71; 62 + 30 = 92; 73 + 20 = 93; 50 + 44 = 94; 60 + 13 = 73; 40 + 34 = 74
Other suitable additions are possible.
Step 3:
From top left, left to right: 63; 81; 91; 82; 92; 81; 95; 48; 77; 71; 55; 83

Test 36

Step 1:
From top left, left to right: 34; 57; 17; 45; 21; 28; 44; 19
Step 2:
From top left, left to right: 80 – 28 = 52; 80 – 27 = 53; 80 – 25 = 55; 67 – 20 = 47; 68 – 20 = 48; 69 – 20 = 49; 90 – 22 = 68; 70 – 25 = 45
Other suitable subtractions are possible.
Step 3:
From top left, left to right: 7; 19; 28; 49; 44; 16; 19; 25; 29; 47; 28; 17

Test 37

Step 1:
From top left, left to right: 61; 90; 82; 71; 39; 19; 16; 16
Step 2:
From top left, left to right: 50 + 42 = 92; 35 + 50 = 85; 21 + 70 = 91; 50 + 19 = 69; 70 – 21 = 49; 67 – 30 = 37; 80 – 55 = 25; 90 – 37 = 53
Other suitable additions and subtractions are possible.
Step 3:
From top left, left to right: 38; 61; 39; 87; 59; 47; 73; 82; 18; 93; 27; 53

Test 38

Step 1:
From top left, left to right: 62; 26; 85; 8; 34; 33; 65; 39
Step 2:
From top left, left to right: 31; 49; 28; 39; 54; 15; 27; 47; 38; 25; 29; 48; 66; 59; 34; 36

Step 3:
From top left, left to right: <; >; =; >; <; =; >; <

Test 39

Step 1:
From top left, left to right: 13; 17; 14; 18; 22; 25; 23; 20
Step 2:
From top left, left to right: >; <; =; =; <; >; =; <; <; >
Step 3:
From top left, left to right: 54; 92; 77; 23; 15; 53; 33; 94

Test 40

Step 1:
From top left, left to right: £21; £18; £15; £18; 13p; 20p; 18p; 17p
Step 2:
From top left, left to right: >; <; >; <; = >; =; <
Step 3:
From top left, left to right: £47; £68; £95; £29; 19p; 71p; 52p; 83p

Test 41

Step 1:
From top left, left to right: 71 km; 72 km; 74 km; 72 km; 93 km; 94 km
Step 2:
From top left, left to right: £20; £18; £20; £20; £26; £28; £24; £19; £17; £22
Step 3:
1. £37
2. £48
3. £38
4. £67

Test 42

Step 1:
From top left, left to right: 85, 85; 95, 95; 92, 92; 92, 92; 94, 94; 86, 86
Step 2:
1. 34 + 25 = 59
2. 16 + 67 = 83
3. 37 + 58 = 95
4. 25 + 47 = 72
5. 24 + 59 = 83
6. 47 + 29 = 76
7. 68 + 23 = 91
8. 18 + 75 = 93
9. 35 + 43 = 78
10. 68 + 18 = 86
11. 16 + 83 = 99
12. 44 + 37 = 81

Step 3:
1. 83; 83; 83; 83
2. 86; 86; 86; 27, 86
3. 98; 98; 98; 58, 98
4. 91; 42, 91; answers will vary; answers will vary

Test 43

Step 1:
From top left, left to right: 46 + 35 = 81; 36 + 57 = 93; 58 + 29 = 87; 14 + 78 = 92; 28 + 67 = 95; 49 + 26 = 75
Other suitable additions are possible.
Step 2:
1. 47 + 36 = 37 + 46 = 33 + 50 = 83
2. 56 + 29 = 26 + 59 = 30 + 55 = 85
3. 31 + 58 = 61 + 28 = 49 + 40 = 89
4. 34 + 52 = 30 + 56 = 26 + 60 = 86
5. 48 + 50 = 60 + 38 = 58 + 40 = 98
6. 60 + 29 = 70 + 19 = 59 + 30 = 89
7. 30 + 46 = 16 + 60 = 20 + 56 = 76
8. 30 + 54 = 24 + 60 = 34 + 50 = 84

Step 3:
1. 86; 86; 86; answers will vary
2. 78; 78; 78; answers will vary
3. 91; 91; 91; answers will vary
4. 97; 97; 97; answers will vary

Test 44

Step 1:
1. Circled: 13, 21, 35, 47, 49, 85, 79, 57
2. Circled: 88, 46, 54, 42, 92, 98, 34, 64, 74, 70, 2, 100

Step 2:
1. From top left, left to right: 5, 7, 9; 15, 17, 19; 33, 35, 37; 51, 53, 55, 57, 59; 77, 79, 81, 83; 85, 87, 89, 91
2. From top left, left to right: 2, 4, 6; 14, 16, 18; 26, 28; 42, 44, 46, 48; 66, 68, 70, 72; 90, 92, 94, 96

Step 3:
1. 82, 27 **2.** 68, 17 **3.** 64, 15 **4.** 80, 43

Test 45

Step 1:
From top left, left to right: 6; 9; 16; 20; 18; 21; 12; 24; 12; 27; 28; 40
Step 2:
From top left, left to right: $4 \times 2 = 8$; $3 \times 4 = 12$; $4 \times 3 = 12$; $5 \times 1 = 5$; $4 \times 5 = 20$; $3 \times 7 = 21$; $3 \times 9 = 27$; $4 \times 8 = 32$; $5 \times 6 = 30$; $5 \times 7 = 35$; $7 \times 1 = 7$; $3 \times 3 = 9$; $8 \times 5 = 40$; $2 \times 8 = 16$
Step 3:
$9 \times 3 = 27$; $7 \times 8 = 56$; $4 \times 10 = 40$; $8 \times 9 = 72$; $8 \times 12 = 96$

Answers

Test 46

Step 1:

From top left, left to right: 1; 4; 9; 16; 25; 0; 6; 4

Step 2:

1. 12, 12
2. $4 \times 3 = 12$, $3 \times 4 = 12$
3. $5 \times 1 = 5$, $1 \times 5 = 5$
4. $5 \times 4 = 20$, $4 \times 5 = 20$
5. $3 \times 5 = 15$, $5 \times 3 = 15$
6. $4 \times 6 = 24$, $6 \times 4 = 24$
7. $4 \times 7 = 28$, $7 \times 4 = 28$

Step 3:

1. 12; $3 + 3 + 3 + 3 = 12$
2. $2 + 2 + 2 + 2 + 2 = 10$; $5 + 5 = 10$
3. $6 + 6 + 6 + 6 = 24$; $4 + 4 + 4 + 4 + 4 + 4 = 24$

Test 47

Step 1:

From top left, left to right: 6; 20; 40; 15; 30; 8; 50; 12; 30; 70

Step 2:

From top, left to right:

five 2s, 5 times 2, $5 \times 2 = 10$;

four 10s, 4 times 10, $4 \times 10 = 40$;

eight 2s, 8 times 2, $8 \times 2 = 16$;

six 10s, 6 times 10, $6 \times 10 = 60$;

five 5s, 5 times 5, $5 \times 5 = 25$

Step 3:

From top, left to right:

10, $2 \times 5 = 10$, $5 \times 2 = 10$;

30, $3 \times 10 = 30$, $10 \times 3 = 30$;

10, $5 \times 2 = 10$, $2 \times 5 = 10$;

35, $7 \times 5 = 35$, $5 \times 7 = 35$;

70, $7 \times 10 = 70$, $10 \times 7 = 70$;

40, $8 \times 5 = 40$, $5 \times 8 = 40$;

20, $10 \times 2 = 20$, $2 \times 10 = 20$

Test 48

Step 1:

From top left, left to right: 80; 40; 90; 14; 16; 50

Step 2:

From top, left to right:

nine 5s, 9 times 5, $9 \times 5 = 45$;

nine 2s, 9 times 2, $9 \times 2 = 18$;

seven 5s, 7 times 5, $7 \times 5 = 35$;

ten 2s, 10 times 2, $10 \times 2 = 20$;

nine 10s, 9 times 10, $9 \times 10 = 90$

Step 3:

From top, left to right:

40, $8 \times 5 = 40$, $5 \times 8 = 40$;

80, $8 \times 10 = 80$, $10 \times 8 = 80$;

14, $7 \times 2 = 14$, $2 \times 7 = 14$;

100, $10 \times 10 = 100$, $10 \times 10 = 100$;

50, $10 \times 5 = 50$, $5 \times 10 = 50$;

18, $9 \times 2 = 18$, $2 \times 9 = 18$

Test 49

Step 1:

From top, left to right:

3, 5, 15

2, 10, 20

2, 5, 10

5, 4, 20

10, 5, 50

Step 2:

From left to right:

$2 \times 5 = 10$, $5 \times 2 = 10$;

$3 \times 10 = 30$, $10 \times 3 = 30$;

$2 \times 7 = 14$, $7 \times 2 = 14$;

$4 \times 5 = 20$, $5 \times 4 = 20$;

$5 \times 10 = 50$, $10 \times 5 = 50$

Step 3:

From top left, left to right: 8; 30; 70; 18; 40; 90

Test 50

Step 1:

From top left, left to right: 20; 70; 50; 80; 50; 60; 70; 80; 30; 20; 40

Step 2:

From top left, left to right: 10; 20; 30; 40; 50; 60; 70; 80; 90; 100; 10; 20; 30; 40; 50; 60; 110; 80; 120; 0

Step 3:

From top left, left to right: 32; 55; 99; 76; 68; 111; 116; 90; 48

Test 51

Step 1:

From top left, left to right: 40; 60; 50; 30; 0; 40; 20; 90; 30; 10; 30

Step 2:

From top left, left to right: 40; 60; 40; 80; 90; 70; 20; 0; 10; 30; 110; 10; 120; 20; 50; 70; 60; 30; 100; 50

Step 3:

From top left, left to right: 74; 25; 57; 99; 45; 64; 96; 77; 48

Test 52

Step 1:

From top left, left to right: 40; 30; 80; 55; 100; 70; 35; 25; 15; 10

Step 2:
From top left, left to right: 5; 10; 15; 20; 25; 30; 35; 40; 45; 50; 5; 10; 15; 20; 0; 35; 55; 40; 45; 60
Step 3:
From top left, left to right: 50; 20; 10; 20; 110; 100; 40; 0; 80; 0; 0; 45

Test 53
Step 1:
From top left, left to right: 45; 5; 80; 40; 70; 35; 50; 100; 45; 55
Step 2:
From top left, left to right: 20; 30; 25; 40; 60; 45; 35; 40; 55; 50; 5; 10; 45; 50; 5; 10; 60; 15; 30; 0
Step 3:
From top left, left to right: 27; 33; 15; 11; 17; 43; 7; 5; 44; 19; 100; 10

Test 54
Step 1:
From top left, left to right: 55; 25; 95; 75; 20; 20; 85; 55; 40; 55; 50; 65
Step 2:
From top left, left to right: 40; 60; 15; 80; 35; 90; 30; 110; 40; 15; 50; 25; 90; 5; 45; 0; 9; 12; 11; 4
Step3:
From top left, left to right: 103; 83; 41; 48; 64; 10; 35; 2; 40

Test 55
Step 1:
From top left, left to right: 25; 35; 40; 60; 65; 45; 60; 90; 85; 55; 95; 25
Step 2:
From top left, left to right: 35; 15; 40; 10; 110; 30; 80; 20; 50; 40; 120; 90; 25; 55; 30; 60; 0; 1; 10; 10
Step 3:
From top left, left to right: 61; 97; 49; 43; 71; 78; 80; 0; 50

Test 56
Step 1:
From top left, left to right: 0; 8; 8; 22; 10; 4; 14; 14; 6; 8; 24
Step 2:
From top left, left to right: 8; 10; 6; 16; 12; 18; 12; 20; 16; 6; 18; 14; 14; 2; 24; 0; 10; 20; 22; 2
Step 3:
From top left, left to right: 2; 3; 8; 2; 12; 3; 2; 11; 5

Test 57
Step 1:
From top left, left to right: 4; 10; 30; 14; 20; 8; 0; 18; 4; 8; 16
Step 2:
From top left, left to right: 12; 14; 24; 8; 18; 12; 20; 2; 24; 16; 6; 18; 10; 22; 16; 22; 5; 12; 2; 12
Step 3:
From top left, left to right: 10; 19; 29; 100; 30; 53; 24; 6; 7

Test 58
Step 1:
From top left, left to right: 21; 34; 52; 41; 61; 58; 50; 81; 31; 43
Step 2:
From top left, left to right: 20; 20; 50; 6; 40; 60; 14; 30; 20; 16; 20; 100; 16; 25; 90; 14; 45; 18; 12; 30
Step 3:
From top left, left to right: 8, 2; 3, 5; 4, 10; 2, 6; 5, 7; 10, 9; 2, 7; 5, 9; 10, 10

Test 59
Step 1:
From top left, left to right: 30; 40; 50; 90; 39; 63; 24; 82
Step 2:
From top left, left to right: 12; 35; 40; 10; 15; 80; 8; 40; 50; 12; 0; 0; 14; 20; 20; 0; 55; 16; 60; 110
Step 3:
From top left, left to right: 10, 2; 5, 8; 8, 10; 2, 9; 5, 4; 5, 10; 1, 8; 6, 5; 10, 10

Test 60
Step 1:
From top left, left to right: 40; 10; 40; 18; 15; 14; 14; 34; 54
Step 2:
1. 0, 2
2. 0, 5
3. 0, 5
4. 0, 10
5. 0, 2
6. 0, 5
7. 0, 10
8. 0, 2
9. 0, 10
Step 3:
From top left, left to right: 3; 2; 2; 2; 7; 10; 2; 1; 1; 2; 3; 4

Answers

Test 61

Step 1:

From top left, left to right: 80; 40; 12; 30; 16; 60; 30; 58; 100

Step 2:

1. 0, 9
2. 0, 8
3. 0, 7
4. 0, 9
5. 0, 9
6. 0, 10

Step 3:

From top left, left to right: 10, 5, 2; 10, 5, 2; 10, 5; 10, 5

Test 62

Step 1:

From top left, left to right: 16; 40; 90; 30; 11; 14; 55; 16

Step 2:

1. 6, 2, 3
2. 8, 4, 2
3. 20, 4, 5
4. 18, 9, 2
5. 40, 5, 8
6. 70, 10, 7
7. 15, 5, 3
8. 60, 6, 10
9. 35, 7, 5
10. 80, 8, 10
11. 45, 9, 5
12. 20, 10, 2

Step 3:

From top left, left to right: 2; 6; 4; 8; 7; 7; 8; 10

Test 63

Step 1:

From top left, left to right: 30; 50; 18; 70; 59; 48; 42; 3

Step 2:

From top left, left to right: 2; 1; 3; 9; 4; 2; 6; 7; 7; 8; 10; 10; 7; 8; 5; 12; 12; 9; 11; 11

Step 3:

From top left, left to right: 18; 24; 57; 71; 15; 34; 70; 21; 80

Test 64

Step 1:

From top left, left to right: 20; 30; 16; 100; 2; 4; 0; 8

Step 2:

From top left, left to right: 0; 0; 0; 8; 1; 0; 1; 1; 0; 0; 30; 0; 34; 77; 1; 15

Step 3:

From top left, left to right: =; >; =; <; <; <; >; =; <

Test 65

Step 1:

From top left, left to right: 20; 29; 50; 0; 60; 14; 40; 60

Step 2:

From top left, left to right: 35; 0; 7; 40; 10; 0; 0; 35; 7; 14; 5; 0; 10; 10; 6; 20; 8; 16; 9; 0

Step 3:

From top left, left to right: 5; 35; 5; 90; 14; 8; 0; 20; 16

Test 66

Step 1:

From top left, left to right: 23; 8; 91; 64; 35; 4; 60; 80

Step 2:

From top left, left to right: 4; 2; 8; 80; 10; 0; 0; 90; 7; 0; 50; 0; 9; 9; 0; 1; 20; 50; 16; 90

Step 3:

From top left, left to right: 7; any number; 0; 6; 5; 70; 1; 4; 10

Test 67

Step 1:

From top left, left to right: 73; 97; 19; 53; 80; 15; 10; 70; 20; 50; 0; 16

Step 2:

From top left, left to right: 10; 3; 2; 20; 5; 0; 10; 8; 0; 40; 0; 1; 5; 10; 8; 9; 56; 0; 32; 95

Step 3:

From top left, left to right: >; >; <; =; =; <; >; <; >

Test 68

Step 1:

1. 12, 12
2. 20, 20
3. 70, 70
4. 16, 16
5. 45, 45
6. 90, 90

Step 2:

From top left, left to right: 5, 15; 10, 40; 2, 14; 10, 60; 5, 35; 2, 18; 8, 10, 80; 2, 4, 8; 8, 5, 40; 2, 10, 20; 6, 5, 30; 5, 10, 50

Step 3:

From top left, left to right: 5, 45, 9; 2, 16, 8; 10, 30, 3; 2, 12, 6; 10, 90, 9; 5, 35, 7; 10, 70, 7; 5, 40, 8

Test 69

Step 1:

From top left, left to right: yes; yes; no; no; no; yes; no; yes

Step 2:

From top left, left to right:

1. 13, 19; 7, 35; 26, 56; 9, 90; 34, 42; 2, 14
2. 5; 96; 15; 2; 60

Step 3:

1. 4, 13, 5, 2
2. 8, 75, 2, 10
3. 0, 62, 4, 20
4. 5, 83, 2, 12

Test 70

Step 1:

1. 23, 14, 9
2. 33, 27, 6
3. 44, 39, 5
4. 63, 27, 36

Step 2:

From top left, left to right: 14; 7; 73; 92; 82; 48; 66; 48; 14; 67; 92; 93; 14; 46; 85; 83; 28; 56; 29; 29

Step 3:

From top left, left to right: 14; 19; 2; 99; 47; 27; 69; 83; 10

Test 71

Step 1:

From top left, left to right: 21; 60; 42; 41; 43; 69; 39; 76; 46; 88

Step 2:

From top left, left to right: 92; 35 + 50 = 85; 21 + 70 = 91; 51 + 20 = 71; 30 + 62 = 92; 80 + 10 = 90; 28; 49 – 20 = 29; 78 – 60 = 18; 69 – 20 = 49; 68 – 40 = 28; 84 – 50 = 34

Other suitable additions/subtractions are possible.

Step 3:

From top left, left to right: 38; 27; 39; 42; 82; 71; 73; 29; 39; 75

Test 72

Step 1:

From top left, left to right: 36; 29; 40; 31; 69; 77; 64; 38; 48; 67

Step 2:

From top left, left to right: 42 + 20 = 62; 21 + 20 = 41; 51 + 20 = 71; 22 + 70 = 92; 20 + 42 = 62; 48 – 10 = 38; 79 – 20 = 59; 38 – 30 = 8; 50 + 24 = 74; 32 + 20 = 52; 68 – 30 = 38; 97 – 40 = 57

Other suitable additions/subtractions are possible.

Step 3:

From top left, left to right: 13; 61; 18; 76; 19; 95; 84; 67; 9; 25

Test 73

Step 1:

From top left, left to right: 54; 30; 76; 19; 35; 30; 66; 40; 40; 95; 85

Step 2:

From top left, left to right: 16; 50; 8; 3; 30; 31; 30; 31; 42; 53; 54; 21; 42; 25; 61; 36

Step 3:

From top left, left to right: 19; 36; 7; 12; 38; 0; 35; 29; 20; 69; 35

Test 74

Step 1:

1. 70, 70, 41, 29
2. 81, 81, 53, 28
3. 38, 92
4. 98, 24

Step 2:

From top left, left to right: 28; 62; 21; 21; 45; 21; 21; 9; 30; 33; 37; 76; 80; 75; 30; 29

Step 3:

From top left, left to right: 75; 93; 91; 24; 18; 0; 100; 24; 68; 23; 96

Test 75

Step 1:

From top left, left to right: 48; 16; 35; 64; 3; 10; 74; 42; 61; 8; 6; 70

Step 2:

From top left, left to right: 40; 40; 7; 7; 20; 16; 5; 9; 80; 10; 9; 3; 40; 60; 9; 8; 45; 100; 6; 7

Step 3:

From top left, left to right: 51; 4; 31; 78; 14; 26; 99; 1; 78

Test 76

Step 1:

From top left, left to right: 43; 24; 8; 14; 10; 4; 17; 19; 75; 6; 5; 25

Step 2:

From top left, left to right: 30; 8; 5; 4; 60; 2; 3; 6; 5; 10; 1; 1; 63; 83; 100; 0; 62; 37; 5; 25

Step 3:

From top left, left to right: 70; 55; 2; 18; 88; 90; 91; 18; 100

Answers

Test 77

Step 1:

From top left, left to right: 40; 49; 0; 0; 1; 6; 32; 45; 50; 2; 2; 10

Step 2:

From top left, left to right: 20; 5; 10; 2; 43; 4; 77; 8; 81; 11; 8; 86; 65; 4; 97; 60; 40; 9; 77; 91

Step 3:

From top left, left to right: 10; 2; 5; 10; 4; 2; 10; 10

Test 78

Step 1:

From top left, left to right: 25; 35; 12; 30; 35; 4; 81; 65; 12; 35

Step 2:

From top left, left to right:

1. 2; 25; 4; 17; 89; 66; 27; 70

2. 10; 2; 8; 5; 10; 5; 5; 10

Step 3:

From top left, left to right: 0; 8; 2; 5; 2, 5 (or 5, 2) or 10, 1 (or 1, 10); 2; 45; 10; 5, 5

Test 79

Step 1:

First table, totals from top to bottom: 20; 30; 40
Second table, totals from top to bottom: 12; 18; 90

Step 2:

From top left, left to right: 2 bags of 8 beads; 4 bags of 10 beads; 2 bags of 10 beads; 5 bags of 9 beads; 6 bags of 2 beads; 8 bags of 5 beads; 5 bags of 10 beads; 2 bags of 8 beads; 5 bags of 8 beads; 10 bags of 3 beads

Step 3:

1. 13

2. 15

3. 24

4. 23

Test 80

Step 1:

From top left, left to right: 10; 2; 6; 9; 6; 9

Step 2:

From top left, left to right: 7; 8; 8; 10; 2; 5; 10; 10; 5; 10

Step 3:

1. £3

2. £18

3. £22

4. £37

5. £63

6. £60

Notes